PRAISE FOR *FORWARD, TOGETHER*

Forward, Together speaks to the heart of what it means to lead and learn in community. George Couros captures both the challenges and the hope of this work with honesty, humility, and heart. His words remind us that real leadership begins with reflection, grows through connection, and inspires the kind of collective purpose that helps every learner and every leader thrive.

—**Jason Fulmer,** founder, Dream Developer Network, National Teacher of the Year Finalist, and South Carolina Teacher of the Year

Nobody gets away with telling the truth about school like George Couros can. As a teacher, it's refreshing to read something real about how to manage the friction between adults at school. *Forward, Together* is funny, human, and sometimes uncomfortably accurate. If you want to move your school forward without relying on fear, frustration, or force, read this hopeful book.

—**Mike Kleba,** SXSWEDU advisory board, NYEdTech Meetup cohost, and author

Forward, Together is George at his very best—wrapping powerful challenges in stories so familiar that you can't help but see yourself in them. What makes this book so compelling is that it calls us not just to lead better, but to see people better. The six principles he lays out aren't abstract ideas; they're lived experiences. An anchor for anyone leading in schools.

—**Joe Sanfelippo, PhD,** retired superintendent, author, and speaker

Forward, Together is one of those books that makes you slow down and rethink what leadership actually feels like in schools and communities. George shows how real growth happens when leaders create space for people to feel seen, valued, and part of the story. That idea shows up again and again through the principles and perspectives he shares, and it's hard not to find yourself reflecting on your own role as you read. If you care about connection, shared ownership, and helping your people move forward together, this book deserves a place on your shelf.

—**Dr. Amber Teamann,** Executive Director of Technology & Innovation

Forward, Together is exactly the book education needs right now. George Couros shares powerful principles that help us better understand others and recognize the impact we have on them. Through heartfelt stories and authentic perspectives, he brings these principles to life in a way that both inspires and challenges without ever making the reader feel judged. George has a gift for drawing readers in and sparking deep reflection, helping us embrace our differences and move forward with empathy and purpose. This book is an invitation to strengthen our connections, honor each other's humanity, and truly move forward, together.

—**Allyson Apsey,** educational leader, author, and national keynote speaker

A clarion call to choose doing what's right over being right. *Forward, Together* empowers us to bridge divides and build stronger connections. Through vulnerable storytelling, practical principles, and reflection that drives action, Couros helps educators and leaders reconnect with purpose and move their school communities forward with clarity and courage. No matter where your community is on its journey, this is an absolutely necessary read!

—**Lainie Rowell,** bestselling author, award-winning educator, and international keynote speaker

As always, George is raw and vulnerable as he shares his own change process and leadership, and this book is truly both a warm bath and a cold shower. (You will have to read the book to get that analogy, and it is one of many keepers!) It nurtures leaders while splashing us with the reality of the changing world we are preparing our colleagues and students for. If you know George, you can literally hear him talking as you read. It is inspirational, at times laugh-out-loud funny, and always grounded in both experience and heart. I read it in a single sitting!

—**Katie Novak,** educational consultant and author of sixteen books, including *The Shift to Student-Led* and *Elevating Educational Design with AI*

George Couros has long been a trusted voice for reimagining what's possible in our schools, and in *Forward, Together* he brings that same spirit of innovation to one of the most urgent challenges we face: how to move forward in a time of deep division. Through honest storytelling, practical principles, and a deep belief in the power of community, George reminds us that progress doesn't come from winning arguments, but from building trust, fostering connection, and working side by side. This is a must-read for educators and leaders who want to not only navigate contentious times but emerge stronger, together.

—**Jill Siler,** leader, speaker, and author of *Thrive Through the Five*

George Couros doesn't offer a one-size-fits-all formula; instead, he gives us timeless principles paired with honest, story-driven perspectives that help leaders navigate the real, messy work of bringing people together. George openly shares both successes and failures, reminding us that leadership isn't about perfection, it's about continually recalibrating, reflecting, and reconnecting with purpose. This book isn't a quick fix, and it isn't meant to be. It's a guide, a conversation starter, and a reminder that the answers we seek are often already within our people.

—**AJ Juliani,** author of *Meaningful and Relevant* and host of *Next Gen Schools* podcast

George has the unique ability to help readers think in new ways and gently push their thinking forward. This book gives you permission to make mistakes, reflect, shine the light on others, and cheer for yourself. Reading it feels as if he is speaking directly to you and guiding you through your journey. I hope this book finds its way into the hands of every educator and leader ready to move their community forward together.

—**Lauren M. Kaufman,** district leader, author of *The Leader Inside*, speaker, and blogger

George Couros brings clarity, compassion, and practical wisdom to one of the most pressing leadership challenges of our time: how we stay connected to one another while navigating complexity, change, and division. This book invites leaders to slow down just enough to reflect, listen, and lead with intention. It does not offer easy answers. It offers better questions that help us build stronger cultures, healthier conversations, and communities rooted in trust rather than fear.

—**Dr. Mary Hemphill,** CEO and founder of The Limitless Leader Collective

While reading this book, I found myself truly recognizing where I am as a leader—something I need to pause and do more often. George's words didn't just affirm my journey; they gently encouraged me toward who I am still becoming. *Forward, Together* is a must-read for anyone striving to lead with heart, courage, and deep connection.

—**Heidi Weeks, Ed.D,** superintendent

***FORWARD,
TOGETHER***

FORWARD, TOGETHER

MOVING SCHOOLS FROM CONFLICT TO COMMUNITY IN CONTENTIOUS TIMES

GEORGE COUROS

Forward, Together: Moving Schools from Conflict to Community in Contentious Times
© 2025 George Couros

All rights reserved. No part of this publication may be reproduced in any form or by any electronic or mechanical means, including information storage and retrieval systems, without permission in writing by the publisher, except by a reviewer who may quote brief passages in a review. For information regarding permission, contact the publisher at books@impressbooks.org.

> This book is available at special discounts when purchased in quantity for educational purposes or for use as premiums, promotions, or fundraisers. For inquiries and details, contact the publisher at paigecouros@gmail.com.

Published by IMPress, a division of Dave Burgess Consulting, Inc.
IMPressbooks.org
DaveBurgessConsulting.com
Vancouver, WA

Paperback ISBN: 978-1-948334-83-9
Ebook ISBN: 978-1-948334-84-6

Cover and interior design by Liz Schreiter
Edited and produced by Reading List Editorial
ReadingListEditorial.com

This book is dedicated to the schools and communities all over the world that work together to create the best opportunities for their children. These communities have proven that when schools and families work together, they double the chance of a child's success. Thank you for all that you do to find the best in each other.

CONTENTS

Foreword xiii
Introduction: Forward, Together 1

Part I: The Principles 13

    Principle 1: Point at Yourself First 14
    Principle 2: Elevate Others to See Themselves in the Story 24
    Principle 3: Build Community 36
    Principle 4: Ensure People Feel Valued 48
    Principle 5: Learn in a Way That You Would Expect from Students 59
    Principle 6: Create a Vision, Together 74

Part II: The Perspectives 83

    Perspective 1: We Are All Somebody's Kid 85
    Perspective 2: Elevating Through Intentional Language 90
    Perspective 3: Listen to Lead 97
    Perspective 4: Somebody Hates You 104
    Perspective 5: Don't Get Used to the Smell 109
    Perspective 6: Learn to Clap for Yourself 116

Moving Forward: Every School Is a Community School 123
Acknowledgments 131
About George Couros 133

FOREWORD

As a school principal, I know the tension of holding hope and hardship in the same hand. Leading a school today means celebrating moments of joy while absorbing the emotional weight of a profession that is increasingly complex.

This is not a book about theory. It's a book about what it feels like to lead in today's schools—with heart, with vulnerability, and with courage. It's about how we stay human in a role that often demands superhuman strength, and more than anything, it's about connection. How we lead with it, learn from it, and return to it. This is not easy work, but it is meaningful, and this book serves as a poignant reminder of that.

From the first page, it's clear this isn't just a book about leadership. It's a conversation with someone who has lived it. The author offers an honest and refreshingly vulnerable take on what it means to lead with empathy, resilience, and integrity. One of the strongest messages throughout this book is the power of connection. Connection to others, to your community, and to yourself. We are reminded that schools are not systems to manage but learning environments made up of people, each with their own stories, strengths, and struggles. George Couros challenges us to listen deeply, to create space for others to be seen and heard, and to recognize that fostering relationships isn't just a soft skill—it's a leadership necessity.

Another powerful thread running through this book is self-compassion. In a role where the wins are often quiet and the criticism can be loud, it's easy to lose sight of your impact. This book reminds leaders that it's not self-indulgent to celebrate our progress or acknowledge our effort; it's necessary. Learning to affirm ourselves isn't about ego. It's about sustainability. When you take care of your own growth and well-being, you're better equipped to serve everyone else in your school community.

At the heart of this book is a deep belief in community. A special kind of community that makes schools not just places where students go but spaces where families feel welcomed, cultures are celebrated, and everyone plays a role in creating something meaningful. That kind of community doesn't happen by accident. It happens when school leaders are intentional about inviting others in, sharing ownership, and building a culture rooted in respect and belonging.

Why should every educator read this book?

Because it reveals the truth about the beauty, complexities, and possibilities of school leadership. It will challenge you to reexamine how you show up, how you lead through hard things, and how you measure your impact. In the process, it will help you remember why this work still matters—maybe now more than ever.

Whether you're a new administrator or one with decades of experience, this book meets you where you are. It will challenge you, affirm you, and most importantly, remind you that you're not alone. It doesn't promise easy answers, but it offers something even more valuable: clarity, connection, and encouragement to keep going.

Schools change when leaders grow and develop.

I am certain that this book will grow you in all the right ways.

—Dr. Rachel Edoho-Eket, principal, author, and speaker

INTRODUCTION
FORWARD, TOGETHER

It's 2011, and I'm sitting in a session at a school leadership conference as a school principal, listening to the presenter discuss the issues with technology in education (and the world) and how schools should not be using it at all.

For the two years prior, I had worked with my school to figure out ways to integrate technology in ways that meaningfully impacted learning and connection and made us more efficient. As you can guess, this presenter's message did not sit well with me.

What did I do?

I pulled out my computer and started blogging.

And not just blogging, but "mad blogging." It's different.

The post I wrote was titled "This Is Not Optional Anymore," and it's a scathing rebuke of the session. Here is a snippet:

> There can no longer be an "opt out" clause when dealing with technology in our schools, especially from our administrators. We need to prepare our kids to live in this world **now** and in the future. Change may feel hard, but it is part of learning. We expect it from our kids; we need to expect it from ourselves.

This is not optional anymore.

That will show them!

My favorite part of the post was when I bolded the word "now" to guilt people into my way of thinking. It was my way of saying to people, "Agree with me, or else!"

To this day, I am both embarrassed and proud of that post. Embarrassed that I once wrote it—but proud that I can revisit it and see just how much I've grown since then. After all, isn't true growth measured by our ability to look back on who we were and appreciate how far we've come? You can actually read the post yourself at the following link (I didn't use Grammarly back then because it didn't exist, so please don't judge!): georgecouros.com/this-is-not-optional-anymore/.

Of course, I hoped people reading my post would see the importance of using technology in meaningful ways for their students and their own learning. That message is one I still believe to this day, and the part about "in meaningful ways" before the term "using technology" is a crucial distinction for the importance of a thoughtful approach.

But it was my tone that was the issue.

The people who already agreed with me probably continued to do so. They were never the target audience. My intent was to reach the people who weren't on my side, and I probably did the exact opposite.

Do you know how I know that? If, even just three years before I wrote it, I had read that same exact blog post, I would have been livid. When teachers, including me, leveraged technology in classrooms in the early 2000s, it seemed to create a disconnect between humans and a connection to robots. I wasn't having any of it, and even though I started off as a computer teacher at the high school and elementary level, in that era in my career, I was as antitechnology as I ever could have been.

THE EDUCATOR PARADOX

Many people in education (including myself) attend conferences looking for ideas we can implement the next day with our communities, while simultaneously disliking the feeling of losing our autonomy and being bossed around. I call it the Educator Paradox: "Tell me what to do, but don't you *dare* tell me what to do."

Case in point: I wrote that post in 2011 to "shame" others into using technology in part because I felt that I was being discredited for using it in my own practice during that session. The blog post was an act of rebellion, and I was James Dean with a bit of a cause.

So, if I was significantly different in 2011 from even a few years prior, how did I change? Often, when we fear trying something new, it's not because of an abundance of information but a lack of it.

Have you ever been terrified at the top of a hill?

In a video titled "Girl's First Ski Jump," a young girl is at the top of a ski hill, filled with trepidation about making a "jump" with a much steeper incline than she has done previously.[1] The view is from her perspective, and you can hear her self-talk and fear as she envisions everything that could go wrong when she makes that jump for the first time. A voice beside her, presumably her dad, walks her through the jump, giving her instructions on how to do it successfully. You can hear the nervousness in her voice. If you watch this video, you can truly feel her fear.

As she summons the courage to make the jump, she does almost a countdown but substitutes the numbers "three, two, one" with "Here, I—"

Right before she says "go," you can hear a faint young voice wisely say, "The longer you wait, you will be more scared."

The young girl says, "Go!" and speedily makes her way down the hill. You can feel her excitement as she lands at the bottom. Upon

---

1 "Girl Gives Herself Pep Talk for Ski Jump," YouTube video, 0:50, posted by CutiesNFuzzies, April 10, 2012, https://www.youtube.com/watch?v=8PN4BC1Aq14.

landing, she says, "It is just the suspense of the top for the first time that freaks you out. That's the only thing! It's so fun! Sixty seems like nothing now! WHOOOOOOOO!"

When I've shared this video with audiences, they thrill in the excitement of the girl landing at the bottom of the hill, but I do my best to point them back to the top of the hill. What made her jump?

First of all, the adult beside her was guiding her from a place of experience and learning. From his coaching, you could tell he had done that same jump several times himself and was able to guide her with an abundance of information and experience. He didn't just push her down the hill and hope for the best! He might not have gone first this time, but he had definitely gone before the young girl he was helping.

And then the young, soon-to-be stoic, sharing her wisdom: "The longer you wait, you will be more scared." That's a crucial reminder that there are things that have become part of our routines today that we once swore we would never do. For example, my high school English teacher, Herman Bauer, would have probably never guessed that I would end up writing every single day. Probably because I told him that I would never write again after high school. Now, I can't imagine going through a day without writing. Pam Allyn once said, "Reading is breathing in; writing is breathing out." This is my exhale, and I don't like holding my breath.

My biggest takeaway from this video is that if you want to move people forward, you have to be the expert guiding the girl down the ski hill who can lead from a place of experience and guide someone in a new endeavor while also remembering you were once the novice who was terrified to make that same jump.

When I wrote that initial post, I tried to be the expert, but I forgot I was once the novice.

If you want to help move people from their point A to their point B, you have to remember you were probably at that point A once yourself. Through a lens of empathy, you are more likely to better understand the needs, fears, and goals of others to help them take steps in their journey and move forward.

Self-reflection and empathy help remind us that we all have experiences of embracing something in our current routines that we swore we never would.

Early on in my school administrator career, a superintendent told us that we all needed to carry BlackBerries. I distinctly remember one of the veteran principals saying at the time, "Over my dead body will I carry a 'phone' with me everywhere I go!" By the time he retired, he often carried two—one for work and one for personal use.

So what led me to jump?

I was skeptical of technology for a portion of my teaching career, and I remember my own brother, Dr. Alec Couros (I just call him Alec), nudging me to use technology in my school. He showed me the benefits, some of the things that he had learned, and helped push me forward without pushing me off a cliff. It was less his words and more his actions that inspired me to do something new and better.

As a professor of educational technology, he knew that my job as a school principal meant we not only had different experiences in education but different roles and strengths as well. My brother made me feel challenged but appreciated (as much as an older brother can do).

THE WARM-BATH-AND-COLD-SHOWER APPROACH

Through the guidance of my brother (and countless others I look up to), I have learned that the combination of having a warm bath and a cold shower is ideal for moving people forward. You want people to feel appreciated and good about what they currently do but also challenged to grow. The importance of this combination is that people do not want them pushing you unless they know you have their back.

In that blog post, I failed to extend the same grace and support that my mentors had once offered me. Instead, I insisted that using technology was no longer optional—a message that landed more like a cold shower than the warm bath of encouragement I had once received.

Do not judge people for not being where you are today when you weren't there yesterday.

MOVING FROM DEBATE TO DISCUSSION

As you read the text above, the conversation in your mind might have been on whether schools and classrooms should use technology or not, or how prevalent it should be in learning. I will not engage in that debate, as it's not the point of this book. In fact, I am not interested in having any debates—which is ultimately what inspired this book.

I was approached by a news outlet to be the "pro-phone-in-the-classrooms person" on a debate for a news show, which I politely declined because I am not "pro-phone." I am "pro-learner," and that's where my focus should be. Now, I do have views on technology in and out of classrooms, and I do my best to engage in discussions, and not debates. The reason I am more interested in discussion over debate is because the latter implies winners and losers, while the former is hopefully undertaken in search of a shared solution.

As Dale Carnegie, author of *How to Win Friends and Influence People*, shares, "You can't win an argument. You can't because if you lose it, you lose it; and if you win it, you lose it."[2]

"Debates" make for great viewing but often create more division than community.

In his book *Intuition Pumps and Other Tools for Thinking*, philosopher Daniel Dennett references Anatol Rapoport's rules of constructive

---

[2] Dale Carnegie, *How to Win Friends and Influence People* (Simon and Schuster, 2022), 112.

argument and debate, which can be used to help frame discussions to move the conversation forward.

How to compose a successful critical commentary:

1. You should attempt to re-express your target's position so clearly, vividly, and fairly that your target says, "Thanks, I wish I'd thought of putting it that way."
2. You should list any points of agreement (especially if they are not matters of general or widespread agreement).
3. You should mention anything you have learned from your target.
4. Only then are you permitted to say so much as a word of rebuttal or criticism.[3]

When we take the time to truly understand someone's perspective before offering our own, we open the door to real dialogue. People become more willing to listen—not because we've "won" an argument, but because we've shown respect, empathy, and a genuine desire to learn alongside them.

Note, the above doesn't work for all situations and that is understood.

But also of note is that if this were used in more conversations, there would be a benefit to all parties that partake, and you are more likely to find the "best ideas" (discussion) than be able to declare "winners and losers" (debate).

Whether it's the "reading wars," technology in the classroom, school choice, or whatever is going on in education or politics at any point in history, the point of this book is not to take a stance on anything but to address a question: How do we move people forward, together? Because if you think about it, any destination in the distance

---

[3] Daniel C. Dennett, *Intuition Pumps and Other Tools for Thinking* (W. W. Norton & Company, 2013).

is much easier and better to get to when we work together rather than in opposition.

As you will see throughout this book, I will share my failures and successes in this process, because if hindsight is twenty-twenty, hopefully my hindsight can benefit your foresight.

PRINCIPLES AND PERSPECTIVES TO MOVE PEOPLE FORWARD, TOGETHER

This book is set up into two distinct parts:

Part one is focused on principles to help you navigate and consider how to move people forward in a somewhat strategic manner. As you learn these ideas, you will need to revisit them and recalibrate continuously.

The principles aren't a "Six Steps to Bringing People Together Formula for Success," but there is definitely some strategic thinking in the process.

Part two is focused on perspectives, through a collection of stories, strategies, and anecdotes for consideration when implementing the principles becomes complex. The reason I felt this was important is that the principles I share are actually quite simple, but that doesn't make them easy. Through sharing some of my failures (there are many) and successes (I even have a few of those!), I hope to help you take stock of your own approach and perhaps learn to step back, connect with others, and bring people together to move forward.

The principles are most important when they are the hardest to maintain. The perspectives can help guide you in holding to those principles in the most difficult of circumstances.

At the end of each chapter, I have provided some questions for discussion, which can be used for your own introspection or, hopefully, to engage with others. These questions are meant to spur reflection, since looking back is one of the best ways to move forward.

An educational leader I admire greatly, School District of South Milwaukee Superintendent Deidre Roemer, shared with me how essential reflection time has been in her own school community. She mentioned that school leaders are often so busy that it takes a conscientious effort to slow down for self-reflection. Leaders and teachers prioritized this step, making time at meetings to write thoughts down and process with a partner. They shared a reflection and an intentional action step that aligned with their strategic plan. She writes:

> It pushes them to be thoughtful about what we are asking staff to do or how we are engaging with families. They know we have to be able to share what we are doing, why we are doing it, how we will know it is working, and where there is an opportunity for feedback. The last one has really helped our staff to take more ownership as they know there is going to be room for their ideas and feedback all the time. We use the process to celebrate success or take small moves between meetings to try something.

She also shared that it reduced conflict between leaders and staff, who were no longer asking why or answering with "That's what we've always done" or "Upstairs wants us to." Self-reflection led to realistic, actionable steps—removing barriers and defensiveness in favor of collaboration.

Deidre's sentiments are why I think taking time to reflect is so crucial in the process of reading this book.

Throughout these pages, I will share some ideas that have worked for me, but if you are looking for a "fix-all" solution, the book will likely be a huge disappointment.

No one knows your situation, context, and community like you do.

You will find answers to your current issues, but not solely through reading. What's most important is reflecting on what would work best in your context.

STORIES MOVE PEOPLE FORWARD, TOGETHER

The pages ahead are filled with stories to hopefully make the ideas stick and create an emotional connection for some of my experiences in the past to what you are facing today and in the future. As Rudyard Kipling wrote, "If history were taught in the form of stories, it would never be forgotten."[4]

But there is also a science behind the importance of sharing, creating, and telling your own stories. According to the article "Your Brain on Fiction" by Annie Murphy Paul, stories can "stimulate the brain and even change how we act in life." It goes on to say:

> Raymond Mar, a psychologist at York University in Canada, performed an analysis of 86 FMRI studies, published last year in the *Annual Review of Psychology*, and concluded that there was substantial overlap in the brain networks used to understand stories and the networks used to navigate interactions with other individuals—in particular, interactions in which we're trying to figure out the thoughts and feelings of others. Scientists call this capacity of the brain to construct a map of other people's intentions "theory of mind."
>
> Narratives offer a unique opportunity to engage this capacity, as we identify with characters' longings and frustrations, guess at their hidden motives and track their encounters with friends and enemies, neighbors and lovers.[5]

---

4 Rudyard Kipling, *The Collected Works of Rudyard Kipling: Volume XIII: Life's Handicap* (Macmillan, 1891), 289.

5 Annie Murphy Paul, "The Neuroscience of Your Brain on Fiction," *The New York Times*, March 17, 2012, https://www.nytimes.com/2012/03/18/opinion/sunday/the-neuroscience-of-your-brain-on-fiction.html?pagewanted=all.

When we see ourselves in a story and make our own connections, ideas resonate and stick.

The hope is that you not only see yourself in some of these stories but also think of the story you want to tell with your community, and more importantly, the story you will *create* with it.

Throughout these pages of ideas, strategies, and stories, I aim to bring people together. Claiming to be the only person who knows how to do so would be the opposite of what I am trying to achieve. That is why your stories matter.

The intention of this book is to initiate productive conversations with our communities, but the answer you are looking for, as Whitney Houston shares, is within you.

If you look for obstacles, you will find them. If you look for opportunities—for and with your community—they might find you.

MOVING FORWARD

Growing up in the small town of Humboldt in Saskatchewan, Canada, I attended a school that was not just part of the community—it was the community itself. I yearn for those days, and I believe that what we had then is not only achievable but beneficial now. As a school administrator, I had many meetings with upset parents, and I would do my best to say things like, "We are both here to do what is best for your child, and if we can work together with that goal in mind, we can at least double the chance of success."

For far too long, we have seen communities, schools, and even families torn apart in society not necessarily because we disagree on where we want to go, but how we get there. This happens not just with our families but sometimes even our own staff. We are so focused on division that we have lost our focus on what is possible when we come together. This book is not meant to focus on what could go (and is) wrong but what we can make right in the present and future for our students and ourselves.

My goal is not to create a vision for any school, district, or community but to share some insights on how you can get to wherever you're going, faster and together.

I would tell you that "this is not optional," but I have already learned that lesson and won't make the same mistake again. That being said, I promise that, in a time of constant contentiousness, we can do so much more together than we can apart.

Moving forward, together. That is the goal.

> ### QUESTIONS FOR DISCUSSION
>
> 1. What is something that you do today that you resisted in the past? What helped you change your mind?
> 2. Who is someone who helped you see things in a different way? What things did they do that you could emulate with the people you serve?
> 3. Think of a time when you tried to move people forward toward something, but the movement was little to none. What did you learn from that process, and what would you do differently today because of that process?

PART I
THE PRINCIPLES

CHAPTER 1

PRINCIPLE 1

POINT AT YOURSELF FIRST

"Maybe it's you?"

Because my focus is on innovation in education, I aim to help people embrace new and better opportunities. However, embracing change for the sake of change is never a good strategy. Seeing opportunities for growth and development is crucial to the improvement of every individual and organization, in that order.

When we complain about the "system" holding us back, it's essential to recognize that the "system" is made up of people, and collective individual growth can significantly impact organizational goals and movement. If we can't improve as individuals, then organizational growth is unlikely to occur.

Once, when a principal learned my focus is on embracing meaningful change, he shared his frustration with me. His staff was not growing, and he was bothered by their lack of progress. He then asked me if I had any ideas on how he could convince them to change their trajectory, or if there were any programs he could leverage to coax their progress. For sure, there had to be *something* that I had experienced in my own work that he could adopt in his.

I responded, "Maybe it's you?"

A confused look came across his face, with a touch of annoyance. He replied with an emphatic, "Huh?"

My reply was the same. "Maybe it's you?"

I then proceeded to share that when we are frustrated with others' progress—or lack thereof—we are inclined to try and change or control their behaviors or perhaps say the things we have already been saying, just a little bit louder. But here is the deal when we are trying to move people forward: You can't change anyone. The only thing you can do is create the conditions where people are more likely to change themselves.

That starts with you.

Not only what you do, but what people *see* you do.

ARE YOU SOMEONE WORTH FOLLOWING?

By my senior year of high school, I had played four years on the varsity team, having been blessed with the combination of an early growth spurt and living in a small town that didn't have enough players to field a football team without enlisting the help of fourteen-year-olds. It was probably more the latter, but I will pretend it was my physical prowess. To be fair, someone once said I was the best athlete to ever come out of Humboldt. Unfortunately, no one else agreed with me, so here I am writing this book.

In my fourth year on the team, the school had just hired a first-year teacher—named Calvin Hobbs (not joking)—to coach us. I was excited for this new opportunity, as I had felt it would be easy to capitalize on my time on the team and create opportunities for myself with a "new teacher" that I might not have been able to get away with under a more veteran educator.

I remember walking into the locker room where he was fixing equipment on his very first day. School had not started, and I was likely the first student he met—not only at this school but probably in his career as a new educator. Excited by the opportunity to make a good impression and benefit from being the first member of the team he'd meet, I went up and introduced myself.

"Coach Hobbs! It's so great to meet you! My name is George Couros, and I just wanted to welcome you and let you know that I am going to be the captain of the team this year."

"Really?" he responded, looking befuddled at my introduction.

"Well, yeah. I have played on the team for four years, so of course I am going to be the captain." I tried to exude confidence in my response, but deep down, I knew I had made a bad impression.

He looked at me and said, "I guess we will see," as he ushered me out of the locker room with his mere attitude rather than his words.

Oh crap. I knew I had screwed up.

That first week of practice was the hardest I had ever experienced in any of my sports. My legs hurt just writing about it. He tested us.

On Friday, the last day of practice, he gathered us together and told us he was going to share the names of the five captains of the team that year. I was nervous to see if I was able to overcome the damage I had done from my initial impression.

The first four captains were named, with my name nowhere to be found. Then he called the fifth, and he finally said my name. I sighed with relief. This is something I had dearly wanted, and I felt vindicated that he saw in me what I felt I deserved at the time.

Coach Hobbs pulled me aside and said, "George, I know you felt you deserved to be captain this year because of the number of years you played, but that's not why you're captain. I named you captain because of your effort this week, and what you modeled for your teammates. It's essential you understand this: You can be ready to lead all you want, but are you someone worth following? That is all that truly matters in leadership."

As he said those words to me, I was overcome with emotion. I took in his words, and, almost with tears in my eyes, I thought to myself, *I don't really care! I am the captain!* His words were lost on me at that moment, although I did try to live up to his advice that season. They came back to me the day I became an assistant principal. I wanted to be someone worth following. This is a good reminder that some of the most important lessons we teach in education do not always stick with our students the moment they are given, but, rather, they may resonate at the point in life when they are most needed. That is why you always teach the lesson.

And as much as Coach Hobbs's words stuck with me, I can tell you I fell short of that standard to be someone worth following more often than I would like to admit.

THIS TIME IT WAS DEFINITELY ME

My friend and I were excited to connect at a large conference. We had lived in different countries, and our time together in person was limited. We'd planned to connect at his friend Dave Burgess's session. I didn't know Dave, and I asked what the name of the session was. It was "Teach Like a Pirate." I thought, *Not really my jam*, but the interest in the session was secondary to seeing my friend, so I headed to the room.

Luckily my friend saved me a seat as it was standing room only, and I am not sure I would have been allowed in if I had entered even a minute later. It was totally packed, not only with people but their enthusiasm. It was palpable and contagious.

As Dave started to talk, I listened and thought, *I totally disagree with a lot of what this pirate guy is saying.* Instead of keeping it to myself, I reached into my pocket and grabbed my iPhone 4 and clicked on the little blue bird icon. My thoughts were about to leave my head and enter the Twittersphere.

For the next few minutes, I started sharing publicly how much I disliked what Dave was saying. Instead of asking questions, I made definitive statements about how Dave's view on education was wrong and mine was right. To me, there was right and wrong on how you viewed education: I was right, and unfortunately, in my view, for Dave (and everyone in that room), he was wrong.

I know better now, but many of the solutions we seek in education are not at the extremes but rather somewhere in the middle. When pendulums swing too far in one direction, unfortunately, they eventually violently swing back the other way.

But I didn't know better then.

Frustrated with what I was hearing, I left the session early and told my friend I would just meet him somewhere later. We met at a local restaurant, and as we entered, he shared with the server that he had reserved a table for six.

"Six? I thought it was just us."

My friend replied, "No, it is for you, me, Dave Burgess—"

The pirate guy is coming to dinner with us?

The second he said Dave was one of the guests, his voice turned into that of Charlie Brown's teacher, and I heard nothing afterward.

I was going to have to sit across the table from the person I ridiculed publicly only a couple of hours previously and break bread with him.

Dave entered the restaurant with sad eyes and slouched shoulders, and he barely said a word the entire dinner. Little did I know he'd received a standing ovation at the end of his session—the happy feelings from which had been quickly extinguished once he'd seen my tweets. The enthusiasm he'd received from many had been dampened by the extreme negativity of one. My messages were not thoughtful challenges. They were rude and judgmental of his views and experiences. I was right and he was wrong, and there was no in-between.

I sat there and saw the destruction I had wrought upon him. I once heard Bill Simmons say on his podcast, "The biggest muscles in the world are internet muscles," and I had flexed mine after flying off the top rope and elbow-smashing Dave's ideas for the world to see. To sit there and see what I had done to another human being was humbling and totally embarrassing.

But it wasn't just Dave I had hurt in that exchange. It was his family who could see what I'd posted. It was people who loved his book while also knowing my work, wondering what I had heard that bothered me so much. It was also the people who wanted to try something new, who then saw what could happen to you if you put yourself out there. While Dave was inspiring people in the room, I was demotivating people online to think twice about sharing their ideas with the world. They didn't just see me criticizing Dave. They saw countless people joining in to agree with my posts. It wasn't just what I said but the space I had created for others to join in. Rather than finding opportunities to move people forward, I had created a space that divided people and created extreme views of what was right and wrong.

There is no doubt in my mind that people second-guessed their enthusiasm about their ideas or decided to not try something new because of my actions toward Dave. By forcing them to choose a side, I also likely turned people away from me and my ideas in the process.

Then I had to see my negative impact in person, and I realized what I'd done. I vowed to never do something like that again and to always do my best to act as if someone I'm interacting with is having a bad day and my goal is to make it better—even when I have no idea what's happening on the other side of the screen. I had spent years as a teacher and administrator encouraging students to "always err on the side of positive," and now I needed to live my own advice.

A CHANCE AT REDEMPTION

About a year after this interaction with Dave, we were both tasked to speak at the same conference. I did not realize he would be there until I arrived, and when I saw him, I was a little uneasy. Although I wanted to apologize, he acted as if nothing had happened and was so nice to me. I was nervous to bring up the incident as it might open a new wound. We had a wonderful conversation, and as we spoke, he said to me, "Have you ever considered writing a book?" I knew that he had just started a publishing company, and I was shocked that he would want to even talk to me, let alone be interested in publishing me. A few months later, I signed a contract to write *The Innovator's Mindset*, and Dave not only became my publisher and chief encourager to get my message out in a way that made sense to me, but we have since become great friends and business partners. As the great teacher he is, Dave advocates to always give students a fresh start, and he has done that for me.

The interesting thing is that Dave and I still don't always agree on many things. But we both know there is space for differing opinions when you have the same goals. We are adamant in empowering teachers, staff, students, and communities to find their own way forward, although we might have different approaches to reaching that destination. It is not our differences that have connected us but our commonalities.

When the goal is the same, the path to get there can be different.

Footprints don't always move forward.

WHY LISTEN TO ME?

As you have read this book, you might be thinking, *Well, this guy is a major screw-up, so I am not sure why I would listen to him*. I get it.

In fact, I remember calling my mom the day I was appointed principal. When I told her the news, she responded in a state of utter disbelief, "You?" She had never envisioned that my time being sent to the principal's office as a child would be an informal mentorship that would eventually lead me to take on the role.

I share these stories with you to suggest that it's easy to point fingers at others first, blaming them for not changing, rather than examining our past and acknowledging our own mistakes that have led us here. As I write this, I can assure you that this is not the end of my writing journey. I know I will be able to write another book in the future, listing all of my newest and most innovative mistakes. More to come in the future!

When you hear about the mistakes of others, sometimes it changes your own behavior. For example, if you shared your frustration with the community by posting negative things on social media about the school, district, or even worse, individuals on your staff, it could create defensiveness that you are infringing upon the right to share their voices. But when I share that I not only screwed up but had to look at the impact of my actions on another human being, it can initiate an opportunity for self-reflection. It is harder for someone to say, "You were horrible for doing that!" because I already owned it. When you make a mistake, it is better to say it first and show how you made it better. Your mistakes can allow others to learn, or they can help them find a new path forward.

As I shared in *What Makes a Great Principal*, "People are more likely to take steps forward on a path if they see footprints from others on the ground."[1] The steps backward and the correction to move forward again are paramount in how we model leadership.

THE IMPORTANCE OF CONFIDENCE IN LEADERSHIP

Sharing our screw-ups can be terrifying, but these stories are less about failure and more about resilience. We all mess up, but we don't all get back up. I share the story about my first interaction with Dave because I have been frustrated with how others act online. We often point to kids screwing up on social media, but I pose this question to you: Have you seen the adults? And do you know who else has "seen the adults"?

---

1 George Couros and Allyson Apsey, *What Makes a Great Principal: The Five Pillars of Effective School Leadership* (IMPress, 2025).

The kids. They are always watching, and they learn more from our actions than our words. Always.

My motivation for sharing these stories does not stem from a place of arrogance or insecurity (although I, like everyone else, deal with these things in some capacity) but rather from a sense of confidence.

In my view, there is a spectrum between being insecure, confident, and arrogant.

Insecurity ←————— **Confidence** —————> **Arrogance**

When I look at those three words, here is how I would define them:

Insecurity is the feeling that you are not good enough.
Arrogance is the belief that you are superior to others.
Confidence is appreciating where you are today, while knowing you can still get better.

When you share your past mistakes, your growth process, and a willingness to learn, it can inspire confidence in others to do the same. Remember: You can't make people change, but you can create an environment where change is more likely to happen.

That environment is more likely to be created if someone can say to themselves, "If they can get better, then maybe, so can I."

MOVING FORWARD

Pointing at yourself first and sharing your growth process can feel scary and risky. We often encourage people to take "risks," but what do we even mean by that?

The word *risk* is often associated with danger, but that is not what I mean.

Risk is simply this: moving from a comfortable average in pursuit of an unknown better.

PRINCIPLE 1

When you look at it that way, taking risks feels a little less challenging—though perhaps still. It's easy to do things the way they have been done, because it creates a sense of comfort.

But is staying the same better? Sometimes yes. If you are doing things that have been done in the past that still work today, keep doing them. In fact, I would challenge you by saying that we shouldn't do new things in education, simply because they are new—only if they are better than what we are currently doing. I don't care about the generation an idea came from; I only care if it works.

But we should never stick with something just because we are comfortable with it, especially if it doesn't work for the people we serve.

If you want others to try something new, they should see that you were willing to go first, risks and bumps and all. In leadership, it's not only essential that we learn but that we are willing to share our process, not just our product.

When you think about it, risk happens when we try new things, yet often the biggest risk we take is staying the same. As I get older, most of my regrets are not things I have done in the past, but things I wish I would have done.

So, maybe you and I *are* the problem? Sure.

But if that's true, our modeling of our own process can be the impetus to new solutions as well.

QUESTIONS FOR DISCUSSION

1. When you have messed up, either personally or professionally, what did you learn from the process that has made you better today? Are you someone worth following?
2. Is there a current initiative or idea that you once resisted and have since changed your actions and thoughts on? What changed?
3. In what ways can you share your learning openly with others so that they can see your progression?

CHAPTER 2

PRINCIPLE 2

ELEVATE OTHERS TO SEE THEMSELVES IN THE STORY

"If your worst ten minutes were online, how many of you would still have a job today?"

That's a question I have asked audiences several times after sharing stories of my own missteps in life. In all the years I have asked that question, not one person has ever raised their hand. In fact, many of the people in front of me start sorting through all of their lives to determine which ten-minute time periods are the worst.

"I would have been fired for that one, that one—definitely *that* one!"

Now, there are many stories I am comfortable sharing with you, but there are way more that I am not. We have all had moments in our lives that we would be extremely embarrassed (at best) to have captured online and made available for others to consume in perpetuity. The point of the question is not only to understand that we are all flawed

PRINCIPLE 2

but also to see *ourselves* in the story while acknowledging that we cannot live up to some of our worst judgments of others.

When you have the spotlight shining on you as a leader, the best thing you can do is turn it around to shine that light onto others.

THE EMOTIONAL CONNECTION TO CHANGE

Just as a spotlight reveals we're all flawed, it also shows the emotional reactions we have to change.

In 1985, Coca-Cola abandoned its proven product to pursue a newer (and better) version, which caused a public relations nightmare.

And people were livid! They hated the new version.

So why would a company do that?

The Coca-Cola company conducted more than 190,000 taste tests on the product, and the new version was overwhelmingly favored over the older version.

So why the outrage?

Because people liked how the old version "felt" to them. The familiarity of the old taste mattered more than the improvement of the new. It *might* have been better, but it *might* not have been.

The company learned that "all the time and money and skill poured into consumer research on the new Coca-Cola could not measure or reveal the deep and abiding emotional attachment to original Coca-Cola felt by so many people."[1]

Simply stated, being better is often insufficient to make a change. We must feel an emotional connection to effect change.

---

1   John Greenwald, "Coca-Cola's Big Fizzle," *Time*, April 12, 2005 (originally published July 22, 1985), https://time.com/archive/6672094/coca-colas-big-fizzle/.

A teacher once said to me, "Teachers aren't scared of change. They are scared of wasting time on things that make no significant impact in their classrooms."

This is true for people in all facets of their lives and across varying industries. Why would I spend my own time doing something different if it doesn't have any benefit to me directly?

As evidenced in the Coca-Cola example, even if the data supports that making a change is better, why would I try something new if I do not see myself in the story? We don't want to admit it, but the thought of *How does this benefit me?* often pops into our minds (or is it just me? Please don't just be me!).

CULTIVATE EMOTIONAL CONNECTIONS AND PERSONAL INVESTMENT

So, then, how do you help foster that emotional connection to try something new?

Show me the value in learning it for myself, and I will teach it to others.

I was recently privileged enough to work with a group of teachers in Atlanta Public Schools, and we began discussing the opportunities for artificial intelligence (AI) and emerging technologies for students. As mentioned earlier, I am always pro-learner first. To be honest, I have my own reservations about new technologies, and there have been many conversations on why you should or shouldn't utilize AI in current classrooms. As the technology gets better, if we aren't intentional in how we use it, it's easy to become dumber in the process.

Strangely enough, my apprehension is part of the reason why I think schools should learn and teach new technologies—so we can guide students from a place of wisdom and experience, instead of playing the game of *Lord of the Flies* and throwing a bunch of kids

PRINCIPLE 2

on Technology Island to fend for themselves, hoping Piggy won't die (spoiler alert: Piggy dies).

But there is definitely a divide not only on AI in education but technology in general.

I saw that was clearly the case as I stood in a room full of about one hundred teachers in Atlanta. Half were excited about the promise of AI, while the other half—not so much.

I had shared my own apprehension about the technology and the possibility of the prevalence of cheating in schools if we weren't intentional with it, which I think many people appreciated. Showing your own fears with any new idea often builds a bridge for people to walk alongside you rather than feeling that they are on their own.

I did, however, mention one subtle way I utilized AI as a new immigrant to the United States. As the tax laws in the United States are very different from Canada, so are your opportunities to invest. Canada has two major basic tax-efficient investing vehicles that are known as a TFSA and RRSP, which basically every Canadian can leverage in one way or another.

In the US, there are Employer 401(k)s, Solo 401(k)s, Roth IRAs, SEP IRAs, and Traditional IRAs. After all my research on these different investing strategies, I didn't know WTH to do. When talking with financial planners, I became more confused the more they spoke. Not all talking is communicating, and although they said a lot of things, it didn't make much sense.

I shared with the group in front of me how all of a sudden it came to me that I could perhaps employ ChatGPT for some assistance, and I wrote the following prompt: "I am self-employed in the US, and want to have X amount of money to live on per year by the age of sixty. What are some tax-efficient investing strategies that I can leverage over the next ten years?"

As I mentioned to the group at the time, being fifty years old (but looking no older than forty-nine-and-a-half, thank you very much!), I didn't want to look back ten years from now knowing I never took advantage of this technology and thus got into a situation where I did not have enough money to live comfortably into retirement.

Most teachers would be frustrated with what happened next.

Every person in the room tuned me out, opened their computers, and began their own financial planning for the future, leveraging AI.

That was the hope.

Instead of telling the audience my views and expecting them to jump on board, they simply saw the value of this new technology for themselves, which made it more likely that they would understand the value of teaching it to students.

I believe that school should be a place where learners have opportunities to find a pathway to success that is meaningful to them. If this were achieved, it would mean that students would walk across the stage at graduation prepared because they have the tools to learn and figure out their own pathways.

My intent with my little side anecdote was not to teach but to inspire learning.

As I shared earlier, teachers aren't scared of change. They are scared of wasting time on things that make no significant impact in their classrooms.

Do you know how others can see something having a significant impact on the classroom? If they see that it can have a significant impact on their own lives. If they see themselves in the story.

THE ARC OF PURPOSEFUL LEARNING

When ChatGPT was released in November 2022, conversations about AI in schools emerged everywhere. Many schools were quick to block access for their students, but ironically enough, you could have probably asked ChatGPT how to get around the filters. For many people (perhaps me included), filters—especially those that block sites that staff and students might see as valuable to learning and aid in productivity—become a puzzle to solve. Of course I believe in blocking sites that are inappropriate for kids, but I once heard that the best filter we can ever provide for students is helping them develop one in their head, and that always stuck with me. If you *block* everything then you don't feel responsible for teaching anything. That becomes someone else's problem.

But as more educators understood the reality that AI was more than ChatGPT and was in tools they had already used for years, the pendulum shifted quickly, and the question they asked was, "How do we teach this to students?" But although it is an important question, many of the responses become questions in themselves or answers to a totally different question.

"Are you sure we should teach this?"

"How is this even beneficial to our students?"

"I didn't use AI when I was a kid! Look at me—I turned out perfectly fine!"

If those are the answers we get to the question, "How do we teach this to students?" maybe we are starting off with the wrong question.

In response to my own feelings on AI and the divide I've seen emerging among educators on this topic, I decided to share my own questions. They are the following:

1. What are the negatives and positives of AI?
2. What are some of the ways that AI can be used in our everyday lives?
3. How can we use AI in our current roles to make our lives easier and improve learning?
4. How can we help students utilize AI for their learning in and outside of school?

Notice that the first question many school communities were asking is a variation of my last one.

The order of these questions matters, and the language is extremely intentional. Let's look at each of them in turn.

What are the negatives and positives of AI?

The reason you start with the negatives is that you create a space to share fears and anxiety about the process.

"Kids will be dumber."

"They will be able to cheat on every assignment."

"The plot of *Terminator 2* will become real, and Arnold Schwarzenegger is too old to save us!"

Let it all out!

As I shared before, I have my trepidations about this and any new technologies as well. The space you create to share these concerns is valuable. As I often communicated with my staff, "I cannot solve problems that I do not know exist."

Creating space to vent is necessary and beneficial. But we need to look at the benefits we might see also. What are some of the positives?

"We can become more efficient in our world."

"This could save us time."

"Robot wars could actually develop character!"

Who knows what answers you will get, but we want to shift our emotions from negative to positive, just like a good story.

In the article "How to Shape a Story: The 6 Types of Story Arcs for Powerful Narratives," Joe Bunting shares the importance of creating an emotional roller coaster through a good story:

> The human brain, though, needs meaning. We need to understand why things are going badly for us so we can avoid it or why things are going well, so we can do more of whatever's working.
>
> This is why humans love stories. Stories give us a sense of purpose, meaning, and shape, and they do that through story arcs. In stories, we get to see the cause-and-effect connections between otherwise random events. We get to experience the deeper meaning in life. We get to see through the chaos of real life and see the underlying pattern.

PRINCIPLE 2

The literary term for this pattern is story arc, and humans love story arcs.[2]

Now, professional learning or community meetings aren't necessarily meant to be like movies or a good book, but why not?

Too often, they seem to be "flat," with an inundation of data and thoughts like, *There's so many other things I could be doing with this time!*

Do you know what else is a flat line? The monitor in a hospital when you are dead.

We need those little blips up and down. They are indicators of life and emotion.

In the same article, Bunting shares Kurt Vonnnegut's description of the "man in a hole" story arc, which embodies that down-to-up progression I'm advocating.

"MAN IN A HOLE" STORY ARC

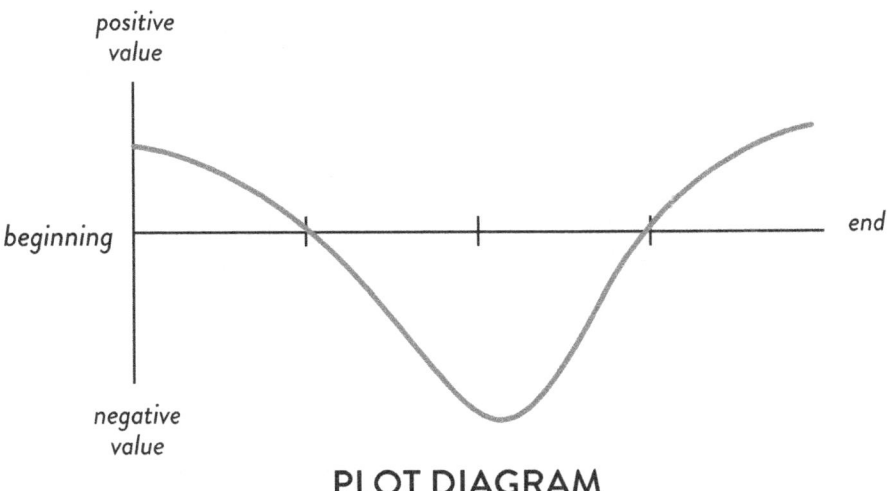

PLOT DIAGRAM

---

2   Joe Bunting, "How to Shape a Story: The 6 Types of Story Arcs for Powerful Narratives," The Write Practice, accessed November 9, 2025, https://thewritepractice.com/story-arcs/.

Do you know when that arc goes up? When we start to see ourselves as the solution to our own problems moving forward.

What are some of the ways that AI can be used in our everyday lives?

Now that we have shared some of the obstacles and opportunities of this technology, what are ways that this can be used in our lives outside of school?

Personally, I wanted to train for a marathon, and I knew there were many plans online but none of them would necessarily work with my erratic schedule.

I decided to create a plan tailored to my life and goals. I asked ChatGPT to make a twelve-week training schedule, with my long run on Sunday and taking Monday and Saturday off from running. It provided a schedule, which I then asked to have put into an easy-to-read table. After that was done, I asked it to convert all measurements from miles to kilometers, because deep down I am still Canadian.

We live in a time where using Google would have been comparatively slow to what I did with ChatGPT—and nowhere near as personalized.

In my weekly newsletter, I shared a few prompts around personal growth that I found from the DailyPrompter threads account that could help with my own health and wellness:

> 1. Workout Plan Generator:
> Design a personalized weekly workout plan based on my goal [insert], my schedule [insert days], and my preferred training style [insert: gym, home, minimal equipment].
>
> 2. Meal Plan Builder
> Create a simple and effective meal plan for [insert goal: fat loss, muscle gain, maintenance] using foods I enjoy [insert preferences] and my dietary needs [insert].

PRINCIPLE 2

Now, plans won't work if we don't do them, but prompts like these could save you time and help you start on a path for personal self-improvement.

How can we use AI in our current roles to make our lives easier and improve learning?

As an administrator, I remember working with my team for approximately a week with giant pieces of paper in a conference room, figuring out class schedules and who would get access to the gymnasium on certain days. We were like detectives mapping out potential suspects and motives to crimes with all of the markers and strings across the walls.

There is *no way* AI couldn't do that in some way, or at least shorten the process significantly.

In my sessions, I will ask people to submit questions to a form. I copy and paste them into a document, and although I spend time perusing the individual responses, I could ask AI to generate a summary of the three main questions I need to address based on learner feedback, which is extremely helpful to the teaching and learning process.

Sharing these ideas in a room full of educators and community members is guaranteed to not only shift their thinking but inspire ideas for their own businesses. When I did an example of compiling information based on surveys in front of a community member who was the CEO of a large company, she immediately came to me and shared how she not only saw the value of it but was going to modify what I did with her own large company.

When we share ideas openly, it inspires action in others.

How can we help students utilize AI for their learning in and outside of school?

You probably now get why this question is last.

If people see how anything is beneficial to them personally, professionally, or, better, both, they are more likely to teach it to students.

The beautiful thing about these questions is that they can be easily shaped for any initiative we are interested in pursuing for our schools. Check out the subtle shift in wording below:

> What are the negatives and positives of using Positive Behavioral Interventions and Supports (PBIS)?
>
> What are some of the ways the process of PBIS can be used in our everyday lives?
>
> How can we use PBIS in our current roles to make our lives easier and improve learning?
>
> How can we help students utilize the process of PBIS for their learning in and outside of school?

Now, I'm not saying you should or shouldn't use PBIS in schools (or even AI for that matter). What I am saying is that when people see themselves as part of the story, they are more likely to want the outcome to lead to a positive ending!

MOVING FORWARD

In his book *The AI-Driven Leader*, Geoff Woods shares something that has stuck with me: "Authorship is ownership."

I often hear people say that it's essential that schools share their story with the world, to which I partially agree. I even wrote the following in *The Innovator's Mindset*: "Sharing our stories about our learning and the ways we empower students helps us make the emotional connections that drive change . . . Stories can become the fuel to innovation in education."

If I could go back and add to those pages, what I would say now is that stories are the fuel for innovation in our schools, but it is necessary to create compelling stories together.

PRINCIPLE 2

If you want to create a compelling story that your community can tell together, people need to see themselves as necessary characters.

> **QUESTIONS FOR DISCUSSION**
>
> 1. When have you felt like an important character in a change effort, and what made you feel that way?
> 2. What are some common reasons people resist change, even when the benefits are clear?
> 3. How can we help others see themselves as part of the story when introducing something new in our schools or organizations?

CHAPTER 3

PRINCIPLE 3

BUILD COMMUNITY

After sharing ideas with groups, I often ask the following:

1. Do you have any questions you want to ask?
2. Do you have any ideas you want to share?
3. And, most importantly, do you want to challenge me on anything I shared?

The last question is one that often surprises the group the most. How often do we share ideas with our communities and encourage them to openly challenge the direction and process of what we are trying to achieve?

Before they challenge me, though, I often share one rule for the process:

"You are not allowed to challenge me at the end of the day, in the parking lot, with your friends, or when I am not there. You have to do it in the room, because I'm not sure if I'm right and I'm always willing to learn. Fair enough?"

PRINCIPLE 3

INVITING PUSHBACK BUILDS COMMUNITY

Let's go back to the idea of the "confident leader" shared in chapter 1. This process can be quite humbling if you feel you are always right (arrogant) or are scared of being proven wrong (insecure). For me, I know that I have much value to share, but I can always learn and grow (confident).

But here is the deal: If you don't ask to be challenged in the room, it's likely going to happen elsewhere, whether you are there or not.

Being challenged is not always a bad thing, but being challenged when you have no opportunity to address the pushback often becomes an issue. Building community is not about everyone agreeing with you. It's better to build things together because we can all have our input and presence in the process.

And the pushback of one might be the same challenge others have. Having the opportunity to address that pushback gives you the opportunity to tackle it head-on or change direction. Either way, you will have more people along for the ride if we can address feelings of discomfort.

Those challenges can quickly become opportunities to not only build community but also people's confidence.

HOW CHALLENGE LEADS TO ENGAGEMENT

I must admit, my hope is *always* to be challenged. For me, it gives me an opportunity to address something I may have missed or could have phrased in a different way. Or, it gives me an opportunity to shift my learning. Whatever the result, I just feel it's an opportunity for me and the room to get better, depending not on what I say but how I respond.

At the end of a talk I did for a group of superintendents and board trustees in Austin, Texas, I asked my "questions, ideas, challenges" questions. A gentleman at the table looked extremely frustrated, and

I knew he didn't want to share a question or an idea: He was going straight to the challenge.

Let's go!

He looked at me and said (as best as I can recall from memory), "You know, you sound a lot like my grandson with all of the ideas you're sharing about technology and AI, and I definitely have some concerns about the direction that schools are going with all of this."

You have no idea how much I loved that challenge. He had said something that I know people are *always* thinking after they listen to me, and now I had an opportunity to address it directly.

"Sir, I totally appreciate that sentiment, and thank you for sharing it. Before I provide an answer, what is your name, sir?"

I will never forget his response.

"My name is James, but my friends call me Rusty. You have to call me James."

Listen, I know I'm an acquired taste. Still, I kind of giggled because I didn't know if he said this as a joke or seriously, but whatever the intent, you just have to appreciate that he would share something so bluntly. My initial read was that this guy didn't like me, my ideas, or both.

"James, I really appreciate what you're saying, and I think it's an essential topic to address. I definitely have similar concerns as you. Can I ask you a question?"

James nodded. I said, "Do you think kids today are better at technology today than you were at the same age?"

"Of course they are!" he responded.

I looked at him and said, "I know this is going to seem weird, but I totally disagree with you."

He looked confused when I said that, as did a big portion of the room. How in the world—with all of the gadgets and technologies of today and how kids utilize them seamlessly—could any adult, including myself, have been better with technology at the same age than they are today?

I then took a calculated guess and said, "James, do you know how to change a tire?"

"Of course I do!" He emphatically replied.

"Well, I'm assuming you are a bit older than me, and as embarrassed as I am to admit this, I would have no idea how to do it unless I used my phone. And even if it got that far, I probably wouldn't use my phone to do anything other than call a tow truck because I have no idea what I'm doing, and over the years, I have become somewhat fond of all my fingers."

He started to perk up.

"Now James, you might not think this now, but changing a tire is actually a use of technology. We just don't necessarily see it that way because we haven't known a world without it. It just 'is.' Even looking back at when I was a kid, I had an Apple IIc, and do you know how hard it was to get that computer to do *anything*? I had to know programming, coding, and so many other things for it to function."

More eyes started to light up in the room.

I then posed the question, "Do any of you remember the manual that came with your first iPhone?" As I watched the group try to think of pulling that paper manual out of their iPhone boxes, I stopped them before they answered and said, "You don't, because it didn't have one! All it had was buttons, and it walked you through everything you had to do!"

As people started to realize where I was going with this, I said, "My contention is that I do not think kids are better at technology today than we were as kids. I *do* think that the technology is so much better today that it can take away the ability to think, and long-term, it can hurt our curiosity and development of wisdom."

I continued, "James, this is why it's so imperative we don't dismiss this with our students. Your wisdom and experience is so necessary in guiding kids on how we use these technologies so we don't become dumber and more disconnected as a community."

He liked that answer, because he didn't just see himself in the story—now he saw himself as a main character. And not because I manipulated him to think that, but because I truly believed what I just shared.

If you want to fix a problem, you address the problem. You do not pretend it doesn't exist.

James now saw his agency in being part of the solution within his school community.

We talked more after the session, and I will admit that I could feel he had taken a liking to me (I am still fifty-fifty since I am a LOT to deal with). But I had an appreciation of him from the moment he raised his hand—because he raised his hand. When we can address the challenges of the community together and work toward solutions that include shared responsibility, we realize how much better we become.

But when I really connected with James was when I received the following email from him a few days later, shared with his permission:

George

I'm sure you hear it many times over after you've done a session about how much people enjoyed meeting you and hearing you speak. Well first off I guess you can add me to that list, however I would like to go a step further. Being 69 years old I hear it more and more from my family about "how set in my ways I am" and how the world is so much different today than in yesteryear. Since returning home Sunday I've now had the opportunity, based on learnings you provided, to point out to my wife, kids, and grandkids, that in many cases things were just as difficult way back when and not necessarily just a "simpler" time as many people now think. When I mentioned the challenges our first computer presented years ago my wife's face lit up like a Christmas tree and that led her to bring up so many other things......

Your teachings were awesome but I also liked the way you "encouraged" challenges and used the challenge as a teaching method and not a "beat down" on why someone was wrong.

Great job and I look forward to possibly crossing paths again someday. I can assure you Santa Fe Texas and Santa Fe ISD will see a difference in me after hearing the world according to George Couros. Thank you.

Rusty Norman

PRINCIPLE 3

Tears. So many tears.

Do you see how he signed the email? With his name reserved for his BFFs, Rusty! EEK! He likes me! He really likes me!

I would like to say I don't cry much, but it's more accurate to say I'm not one who doesn't cry much. As altered from my favorite movie of all time, *Billy Madison*, "If crying is cool, then I am Miles Davis."

But the courage of my friend Rusty, and his willingness to not only challenge but be challenged back and then learn to do something to move forward, is an opportunity that *only* would have happened if I encouraged people to push back.

BUILDING COMMUNITY IS ALSO BUILDING UP COMMUNITY

One of the things that I often share with organizations when I encourage them to challenge me is that it doesn't mean I won't challenge back.

Even in the conversation with Rusty (my friend), I didn't just say, "Yes, sir." I did my best to show opportunities for us to move forward, together. Ironically enough (I was listening to Canadian icon Alanis Morissette as I wrote this sentence!), having the conversation also grew me in the process. I think that is wonderful, don't you think? (Okay, I'll stop!)

As a leader, it's imperative that you share some of your hopes and dreams with your community. In *What Makes a Great Principal*, I shared advice that one of my mentors, Mary Lynne Campbell, provided me when I was tasked with becoming the principal of a school: "What will your fingerprints be on this school? After you leave, how will people know you were there?"[1]

As a leader, you need to know when to stand behind your people, when to guide them from the side, and also when to be in the front. Knowing the right time to do each is part of the artistry of the process.

---

1   Couros and Apsey, *What Makes a Great Principal*.

Donna DeSiato, superintendent of the East Syracuse-Minoa Central School District, is one of those leaders that embodies knowing when to do all three. Having the opportunity to be in her district and work with her faculty, I watched her share something with her team that I can paraphrase now: We must provide permission, support, and protection. Permission is the opportunity to try new things that we aren't sure work yet. Support ensures that professional learning is in place to help educators reach the next level. Protection is ensuring that if things don't work out the way things were planned, teachers know they are safe.

That statement from Donna shows the importance of pushing a community to new heights while ensuring they know you've got their back in the process.

Warm bath, cold shower.

One of the things that really struck me, though, is how Donna and her district are ensuring that, although they do well on them, they know that standardized tests are only a single metric of what they do. I have often said that grades do not tell the story of a child, but too often, the biggest (and seemingly most important) story we tell our community is how well students are doing on tests.

Donna had a clear message: "If we (educators) only focus on standards and tests, why would our parents focus on anything else?"

And she was going to make sure that her fingerprints were on changing that perception within her school community.

Anytime Donna had a school extracurricular event, whether sports, fine arts, learning fairs, etc., she would address the community and introduce the event by saying a variation of the following: "We know that we have state standards and requirements that we are supposed to meet, but that is just one of the ways we show our learning. Tonight, we show another aspect of what learning looks like in our community, and I hope you can see the impact it has had on the students. Please enjoy!"

PRINCIPLE 3

Some of you reading this are thinking exactly what I thought when I heard Donna say that: *That is such a good way to communicate with our families at the beginning of events! I am stealing that.*

As a leader (not administrator, as those are different roles), your part is to lead people forward in a positive manner, but sometimes it's hard to get to moving when you don't have a destination.

The famous quote often attributed to Henry Ford, "If I had asked people what they wanted, they would have said faster horses," is true for so many organizations, including education.

My very close friend Dr. Katie Martin once said, "As educators are working harder than ever, I wonder if sometimes we are getting better at the wrong things. Our system was designed for a different era that was built on standardization and compliance, and is not suited for the world we live in today."[2]

Sometimes when you want to grow the community, you have to show the community a new way and point them to the possibilities of a new direction.

MAYBE YOU'RE WRONG?

Although I am sure you know many things (probably more than me!), we have to understand we don't know everything. Humility is one of the most underappreciated leadership traits, and I have adopted the idea that you need to either be humble or you will get humbled. I prefer the former to the latter.

When I was writing *The Innovator's Mindset*, there was a parent in a neighboring community who was very vocal about how schools needed to "go back to the basics!" and she may have even seemed a bit confrontational. I didn't know if she actually was, but I did know that I didn't want to find out!

---

[2] Katie Martin, "Want to See Change in Education? The Key Is Trusting Relationships," September 20, 2020, accessed November 9, 2025, https://katielmartin.com/2020/09/20/want-to-see-change-in-education-the-key-is-trusting-relationships/.

Writing a book on innovation in a small Canadian town, I thought that I might become a target for her ire and she would go after everything I wrote. My mind is very proactive, not necessarily because I am thoughtful— I just don't like getting in trouble.

So I started digging into her work. At the beginning of writing my book, I was hoping to challenge people to rethink education entirely, suggesting that we needed to go away from the old to get to the new because it was just better for education and, honestly, society in general. But the more I read of what this parent had to share, I started to think that I was definitely missing something. My focus was so much on the aspirational that I forgot about the foundational. Her work wasn't counter to mine, but a complement. Even when you feel you are right, it might not be the right time.

I wrote the following in *The Innovator's Mindset*, and I can credit it to her push in my own learning.

> But what about the basics?
>
> With all of this talk about "innovation" and "twenty-first-century learning" in organizations, some worry that the basic skills of literacy and numeracy will be forgotten. In fact, quite the opposite is happening in many organizations.
>
> Innovation demands that our students learn the basics, but how we go about teaching them may look different than in years past. The basics are crucial, but they cannot be the only things we teach our students. Yong Zhao summarized this nicely when I saw him speak at the 2012 ISTE conference, where he stated, "Reading and writing should be the floor, not the ceiling."[3]

That parent shifted my thinking, which didn't replace my ideas but made them stronger. When I hear people say, "The number one thing

---

[3] George Couros, *The Innovator's Mindset: Empower Learning, Unleash Talent, and Lead a Culture of Creativity* (IMPress, 2015).

employers are looking for is people with AI literacy!" my first thought now is, *Not if they can't read and write.* Foundational to aspirational. Embracing the idea that sometimes you are wrong doesn't make you look weak, but it can, in the long term, make you stronger.

That parent taught me indirectly that when we share the lessons of the past while embracing the opportunities of today, we empower our students to create a better future. We can't create and sustain a community without the necessary building blocks to anchor us and new ideas to grow us.

It is not one or the other; it sometimes can be both.

As a principal, I told my staff if I ever brought something to them for discussion, I was truly open to discussion and changing direction. But, sometimes, the decision was already made by someone else, and we could still talk about it if they wanted but nothing would change based on the conversation. Most appreciated my candor and being up front with what was in our control and what wasn't.

There was one initiative that I wanted to introduce to our school that I thought would be widely embraced by my staff. My thought was that I would bring it up at a staff meeting, we would talk about it, I would convince them of a way forward, and it would just be a done deal. Weirdly enough, I can't remember what it was, but I do remember the outcome.

My staff vocally *hated* what I had to share. They were against it. I will admit, I didn't accept it at first, so I did my best to convince them why my way was better. And then I tried to convince them more.

Nothing.

In that moment, I learned that being a car salesman was not in my future, as I couldn't have given them a vehicle if I tried.

I acquiesced and said, "Although it's obvious I disagree with you all, I promised that if it was open for discussion, it was a decision we could make together. All I ask is that we have the opportunity to revisit this in the future."

They knew I hated the staff decision, but you could sense that they didn't feel like they had beaten the administrator; rather, they felt I had kept my word on what I would do, and it was surprising as much as it was appreciated.

I would like to say I was happy in the moment, but my smile was made up of gritted teeth and I was a pouting eight-year-old on the inside. I kept my word, but I didn't like it!

My assistant principal, Cheryl Johnson, came to the office afterward. She knew I was bothered, and she said to me, "I know you hate what just happened, but I am very proud that you listened and did right by the staff. The trust you just earned is much more valuable than the decision that you didn't like."

She was right (and awesome, which is why I hired her). I started to realize that sometimes we have a vision for where we want to go, but the *we* is imperative in the process. If I had pushed my staff to simply do what I wanted, they might have, and then they might have fought me on everything else and caused issues in other areas.

It's not always a bad thing to step back so that you can lay the groundwork to eventually step forward. Trust is essential in that process.

Sometimes maybe you are wrong, and sometimes maybe you're right but it's just not the right time. Time is the most precious resource we have, and I don't like mine being wasted nor do I want to waste the time of others. Investment in your community is much more valuable, long-term, than any initiative you can implement in the short term.

When building community, it is essential to recognize what you can lose when you are obsessed with winning over *we*.

MOVING FORWARD

As a leader, when trying to grow your community, it's essential to recognize when you need to step aside, take a step forward, or move to the back. No matter how smart you are, there's always something you

PRINCIPLE 3

can learn from and with your community, whether it is students, staff, or families.

But no matter where you are in that spectrum, it's imperative that you respect the experience, voices, and wisdom of your community.

I tweeted the following in 2017 and believe in this idea deeply.

Growing your community means recognizing that although we may disagree, when we work together, we can still find a pathway forward.

When people feel valued for what they have to contribute, they will gladly get on a path with you, even if they feel uncomfortable, as evidenced by my friend Rusty.

When you build your community up, they will in turn make you better through the process. Once they know you see their gifts, they are more likely to give them to you.

QUESTIONS FOR DISCUSSION

1. When have you seen honest pushback help a team or community grow stronger?
2. How do you encourage others to share ideas or challenges openly with you?
3. What is one example of a time when you realized you might be wrong or that it was not the right time to move forward?
4. In what ways can inviting challenges and disagreement strengthen a school or organization's culture?

CHAPTER 4

PRINCIPLE 4

ENSURE PEOPLE FEEL VALUED

Building and knowing your community is a prerequisite for *growing* your community.

However, it's not about growing people into what you want them to be; it's about recognizing their gifts and creating a culture that unleashes their innate potential.

As someone who focuses on innovation, people always see me as the "change guy" in my work with schools, and I am often asked this question: If you were to lead a new school or district today, what is the *first* thing you would change?

My answer today, ten years ago, and ten years from now, will always be the same.

Nothing.

Too often, it's easy to go into a new organization with your own vision of what it should be rather than knowing what it *has* been and what it *could* be. If you go in with a personal agenda of what you want to do, it will become you vs. them quicker than you could imagine. I have seen it in action, been a staff member that experienced it, and to some degree, done it more in the past than I would like to admit.

If people feel you are trying to "fix" them, they will fight you tooth and nail. But if people *know* they are valued, they are more likely to be on your side. To know your people, though, you have to pay attention to the smallest of details.

EDUCATION AND BROWN M&M'S

You have heard the jokes about the brown M&M's when referring to people with outrageous demands or acting like divas. Over time, this story became so convoluted that many people (including me) thought that, at some point, a rock band had asked for *only* brown M&M's, but in fact, this version was wrong.

I was listening to a podcast and I was surprised when I heard the origin of the story and, actually, the brilliance behind it.

The podcast mentioned that the band Van Halen used to make an interesting request in their contracts: a bowl of M&M's was to be placed in their green room before concerts, and all of the brown M&M's were to be removed from the bowl.

Why in the world would someone do this? I mean I can taste the difference between almond and regular M&M's, but I assumed that the red and brown ones had no distinction in flavor (although I am going to try some the second I am done writing this chapter!).

There was actually an interesting reason behind the strange request from the band, as shared in this article from entrepreneur.com:

> Buried amongst dozens of points in Van Halen's rider was an odd stipulation that there were to be no brown M&M's candies in the backstage area. If any brown M&M's were found backstage, the band could cancel the entire concert

at the full expense of the promoter. That meant that because of a single candy, a promoter could lose millions. . . .

To ensure the promoter had read every single word in the contract, the band created the "no brown M&M's" clause. It was a canary in a coalmine to indicate that the promoter may have not paid attention to other more important parts of the rider, and that there could be other bigger problems at hand.

Whenever the band found brown M&M's candies backstage, they immediately did a complete line check, inspecting every aspect of the sound, lighting and stage setup to make sure it was perfect. David Lee Roth would also trash the band's dressing room to prove a point—reinforcing his reputation in the process.

Van Halen created a seemingly silly clause to make sure that every little detail was taken care of. It was important, both for the experience of the fans and the safety of the band, to make sure that no little problems created bigger issues.[1]

Huh. As someone who has been blessed with the opportunity to speak to organizations all over the world, I have been asked if I only want brown M&M's, hinting that I could be a diva. I used to laugh, but upon hearing this story, I share it with *anyone* who will listen because I find it so utterly fascinating, both in how the clause was so misconstrued for public consumption that people rarely understood it (hence why it is essential schools share their own story) but also how essential it is that we pay attention to the small details.

And, if you don't pay attention to the small details, they can become massive problems.

---

1   Steve Jones, "No Brown M&M's: What Van Halen's Insane Contract Clause Teaches Entrepreneurs," *Entrepreneur*, March 24, 2014, accessed November 9, 2025, https://www.entrepreneur.com/growing-a-business/no-brown-mms-what-van-halens-insane-contract-clause/232420.

PRINCIPLE 4

As a school administrator, I would spend each morning greeting staff, students, and community into our buildings—more than just a nice start to the day, this was a way to check in on people and be proactive in how I connected with them. If I saw students playing basketball on the court, reading a book under a tree, or telling some of their favorite jokes (always school appropriate!), it was an opportunity to learn about them and leverage their strengths within the classroom context.

The same was true with the adults. As a principal, it was imperative that I knew my staff beyond their jobs. Little conversations about their interests in music, movies, sports, or other aspects of their personal lives could help me help them excel as professionals.

Too often, we act as though we are educators who happen to be humans rather than recognizing we are humans who happen to be educators.

As the M&M's story suggests, the small details and connections made on a personal level can feel inconsequential, but they can be a way to uncover strengths early and build trust. The little things can always become the big things, and being proactive ensures they end up being big and *good*—because the opposite is no fun at all.

If you want to grow your people, you have to know your people.

STRENGTHS BEFORE INITIATIVES

I remember once reading the sentiment that if an educator teaches something to a student one hundred times in the same way and the child doesn't understand it, it's not the student who's the slow learner.

The same is true in leadership.

If you can't get people to move forward after trying the same thing repeatedly, as mentioned in chapter 1, look at how you are leading rather than blaming someone for not following correctly.

This is said not out of judgment of anyone else but because of my own mistakes in leadership.

As much as I tried to enter a new school community going "slow to move fast" and understanding the people I served and their strengths, I have made several missteps along the way. One of the initiatives I hoped we would adopt as a community was ensuring that every student had the opportunity to create a digital portfolio, not only to showcase their learning in school but also to help them build a positive digital footprint for their future. As you read this, every student you serve will not only be googled but also found through AI agents, such as ChatGPT. Digital footprint was and remains something that I am still very passionate about, and I encouraged my school to adopt this initiative.

My contention was that if we were going to teach students to make these portfolios, we would have to go first as adults, because we couldn't really teach something we had never learned. When we started the initiative, this was very new to not only school but society in general.

Many of my staff members were on board with creating their own portfolios because they not only wanted to learn but they saw the potential for their own opportunities. They saw value in claiming a space online just in case they wanted to apply for different jobs in the future (although, why would anyone ever want to leave when I was a principal? Is it me? Am I the problem?), and they were ready to go.

But one teacher did not see the value in the process, and she fought it tooth and nail. She was not only a teacher on my staff but a teacher with influence on the staff. A scary combination for a principal if they don't like you!

I will tell you her name is Sheryl, and she is not the one who looks bad in this story.

Sheryl fought me tooth and nail on this initiative and did not see the value in the process. I nudged her to not dismiss the process, because she couldn't really understand whether it worked or not unless she tried it. I promised I would back off if she put some actual effort into the process and *then* gave me feedback on why she thought it was bad.

She wasn't having it.

PRINCIPLE 4

Honestly, it kind of broke me. I just couldn't get her to move ahead, and I knew that it would also mean a lot of the other staff wouldn't be interested in trying either. Sheryl had been there for years, and I had only been there for months. When they made calculated guesses on who would last longer, I was the long shot!

As I shared earlier, teachers aren't scared of change, but they are definitely scared of wasting their time on something that they don't think will have an impact on the classroom. Sheryl didn't see it, no matter how hard I tried.

So I threw in the towel a bit and backed off.

One of the things that I used to do as a school and district administrator is go into teacher's classrooms (with their permission), pop open my laptop, and knock off some emails or reports in the back of the classroom. This could take anywhere between one to three hours, and I would also inform the staff that I wasn't there to observe them, but rather to see if there was any way I could help. If you make decisions for classrooms, you better be in those classrooms to see their impact. I recently discussed this with a principal and stated that you could *never* break the trust of the staff member in this process. This was not an opportunity to ever provide negative feedback, even if you witnessed something you disagreed with, unless it was obviously egregious.

When I asked Sheryl to spend that time in her classroom, she had zero hesitation and made a nice spot for me. The chair for a grade-one student ensured my six-foot-four frame would have my knees past my neck as I sat down.

I couldn't help but notice how incredible a teacher Sheryl was. She embodied the idea that teaching was both science and art, and she was both Marie Curie and Picasso. So good. Honestly, she was a better teacher than I had ever been or could be.

Right before I left, I shared my admiration and, as an aside, said, "The whole staff would benefit from what I just saw today! Would you be open to writing something for your portfolio so I can share it with them?"

Without hesitation, she said, "Of course!"

She could tell my genuine admiration for her work and that I knew she could lift the whole staff. I quickly realized WHY she had a tremendous influence on the staff. They had already seen in her what I hadn't been looking for: She was an incredible teacher.

I had focused so much on what she couldn't do that I didn't pay attention to how good she was at the things that I couldn't do.

It would be great to tell you that I knew what I was doing when I walked into that classroom and that I could harness her strengths to move the school forward, but then I would be lying to you. It was after the fact that I realized this, and it changed how I approached not only Sheryl (sorry for sucking, Sheryl, if you are reading this!) but everyone else moving forward.

If I could build on what people were already good at and help them see that in each other, how could that bring our school to become the best version of itself?

THE EXPERT ACROSS THE HALL

As the Van Halen story reminds us, it's imperative that we look for the small details in the people we serve, but sometimes the easiest way to find them is to encourage the staff to reveal those gifts themselves.

My experience with Sheryl helped me refocus on something I already knew. If we could see the details and strengths in each other first as individuals, then the potential growth we could have as an organization would be exponential. Tom Rath, author of *StrengthsFinder 2.0*, shared, "When we're able to put most of our energy into developing our natural talents, extraordinary room for growth exists."[2] The question for me was how to get others to shift their focus on looking for each other's strengths the way Sheryl helped me see hers.

In my second year as a principal, we were looking to revamp our professional learning program. I knew that most of these initiatives had

---

2   Tom Rath, *StrengthsFinder 2.0* (Gallup Press, 2007).

PRINCIPLE 4

failed because they were one-and-done models that were seen as either time fillers or a box to check for your bosses. Once you did it, whether it was effective or not, you were done.

But I wanted professional learning to be an investment that had substantial returns, not only on the content we focused on but also on how we saw each other as colleagues. This would be an excellent opportunity to try something new with my staff that would build on what they were already doing well.

As a principal, I reviewed our data and district initiatives, and I spent a considerable amount of time reviewing information (I would now utilize AI to assist me with that task!). I identified three initiatives that I believed we needed to focus on, and I presented these areas to the staff, acknowledging that I assumed they didn't want to spend their time going through all the extraneous information, but if they wanted to, I could create a time and space for that. To be honest, they had no interest, because they already have a ton of things to do. As a teacher, this was something I honestly had no interest in doing.

That being said, when I shared the three initiatives, I communicated with my staff that if they had any issues with the focus areas I presented, they were more than welcome to push back and share any alternative options they thought would be better. Surprisingly, they immediately agreed with the three areas I presented, but they asked if they could add a fourth.

I hesitantly agreed, not because I thought they were wrong, but because I wanted to limit our focus areas—since, as we know, educators do not only have full plates, but platters, and they are overflowing. Schools struggle with initiative fatigue because we seemingly always add but never subtract. Because I knew this was less about getting their buy-in and more about ensuring they had ownership over the process, I agreed to the addition.

BUY-IN VERSUS OWNERSHIP

Buy-in is often about generating excitement for something the leader wants to do. A person or group of people are all in on participating in an initiative or growing an idea. In the scenario I'm describing, the staff had already bought in to the three initiatives. They were on board. They believed in the ideas enough to be a part of them.

Ownership is more about feeling pride in ensuring success about something you created together. It has to do with personal responsibility and care over a particular idea, task, or result. To feel ownership, not only do individuals need to believe in the ideas to participate, they must believe their participation is integral to the success of the idea or initiative.

Adding that fourth initiative ensured they saw their fingerprints on the process. By taking charge or having ownership over these initiatives, the staff was able to recognize and contribute their own abilities, gifts, and passions.

Now that we had identified the four areas, I asked the staff to join teams in areas they were excited about or felt they already excelled in. Each team (which I joined as an equal member as the principal) would identify areas of focus for the school, objectives for professional learning, and measures of success. The last point was crucial, because they were more likely to achieve the goals they set out for the school themselves rather than goals I decided for them. They had more accountability for the success of the school when they created the measures than if I did it for them.

They created a plan for professional learning for the school and delivered it to the community, instead of having someone else do it for them. What I loved about this process was that it created a bit of competitive collaboration in the school, which I believe creates that push support (warm bath, cold shower) feel among colleagues. When they saw how incredible one team's professional learning day was, they would often want to (competitively) improve their own efforts, but they had no issue asking other teams for help (collaboration). When you create a culture that *pushes* people toward success while supporting them in their *growth*, the big winner will always be your school community, especially the students.

As this process unfolded, there were so many incredible benefits. First of all, we saved money by creating and delivering our own professional learning plan. I spent a portion of that money providing meals on those days—including one that my own mom and dad cooked for my staff. Whether they liked me or not, they would definitely want my parents to come back so they could enjoy their authentic Greek cuisine! It was a great way to invest in the staff.

But the biggest benefit was not on the impact the learning had on the school but the way they started to see each other. If you have been in education for any period, you know there's often a sense of tall-poppy syndrome. The people who stand out for their ideas or success are quietly resented or brought down to size so that no one appears too ambitious. When we focused on recognizing strengths and celebrating contributions, that mindset began to shift. Instead of feeling threatened by each other's growth, the staff started to see individual success as something that lifted everyone up.

Too often, we celebrate experts across the world, but if you want to bring people together, we have to ensure they see the expertise within the community.

I don't remember what the four focus areas were, and now they seem to be irrelevant. Initiatives will come and go, but we remember the shifts that happen when people build something together. The more you can create a community with a shared vision and clear goals that leverages the genius of one another, the further you will be able to go together.

MOVING FORWARD

We don't want our students walking out of school all being good at the same thing. We want them to know they are good at something.

The same is true for adults.

We spend so much of our time trying to make people the same instead of stepping back to recognize that their unique gifts and contributions to the community will actually make us stronger. As the Van Halen story reminds us, when we pay attention to the little details of who we serve, our effort pays off in enormous ways.

If you want to bring people together during contentious times, you have to help them see in themselves and in one another that gifts and passions will not only make us better but also help us reach our shared goals faster than if those contributions were ignored.

Those details matter.

QUESTIONS FOR DISCUSSION

1. What small details or hidden strengths in your school community have you overlooked that, if recognized, could bring people together in powerful ways?
2. How can you create more opportunities for staff and students to share and celebrate their unique gifts, especially during times of conflict or uncertainty?
3. When have you experienced a moment in which focusing on people's strengths shifted the culture of your team or school? What did you learn from that experience?

CHAPTER 5

PRINCIPLE 5

LEARN IN A WAY THAT YOU WOULD EXPECT FROM STUDENTS

As I mapped out this chapter, I realized there are a couple of confessions I need to make.

The first one is this: I am not the biggest fan of "learning norms" (some call them working agreements, shared expectations, etc.) in education. It's probably because they've been forced upon me in some way or another.

Most people hate being told what to do. Even when I know something is good, if I feel it's being pushed onto me, my initial reaction is to resist. I know this is not just me! If it were, I wouldn't be writing this book!

That said, in some professional learning sessions, people have insisted on asking me about my learning norms. I thought about it, and I wanted to find a balance between giving a suggestion and providing a distinct direction while also sharing something that aligned with my own philosophy and offering a direction for where I was going with my thoughts. Instead of working with the group and creating standards together, I shared this one sentence and asked them to commit to it: "Learn in a way that you would expect from your students."

That was it. Now, I didn't define what that looked like for the group (even though I do have thoughts about what it means to me), but I shared it in a way that it was almost a question rather than an answer. I totally Jeopardy!'d the group. (I just made up that term; I kind of like it.)

My hope was that it would spark a conversation with the group and they would start considering questions such as "What do we expect from our students? What does that look like in our classroom? Could we even do what we expect?"

One of my driving beliefs is that the experts are those closest to the work. I have seen the value and impact of sharing my learning to inspire others, but as educators, you're the experts. You are the ones closest to the work in the community, the ones who take new ideas and make them work based on what you know and what's needed in your context.

This learning norm hopefully promotes conversation about what we expect from students and ideally sparks some reflection about what you model as a learner.

Are we, as the adults, learning (and even acting) in the way we would expect from our students?

Kids learn more from watching us than listening, and it's why reactions like yelling, "BE QUIET!" (which I have totally done) might create short-term relief but will develop long-term habits that we might not be too thrilled with.

What we model in our words, actions, and mindsets is what we instill in students.

PRINCIPLE 5

ALL LEARNING STARTS WITH CURIOSITY

One of the ideas schools and districts seem to agree on is that the words that start with the letter C are essential to education. These C words typically range in number from three to eight, and the actual words used vary all over the world. Sometimes these C words are "character, collaboration, creativity, community, critical thinking," but sometimes it's easy to feel we are constantly dealing with "catastrophes" and are burdened with a feeling of "cluelessness" in how to move forward.

Basically, there are a lot of words that start with C that we could use in education.

The one that I was convinced mattered the most was *curiosity*.

Will Richardson wrote an article titled "Curiosity Is the Cat," in which he shared the following:

> I mean really, when it comes to learning, what comes before curiosity? . . .
>
> Think of most skills, all the stuff that doesn't show up on the report card, all the stuff that probably matters more than the stuff that shows up on the report card, and you'll find they are steeped in curiosity. Problem-solving, problem-finding, persistence, cooperation, adaptability, initiative . . . (add your 200 more here). Which of those doesn't require being curious first and foremost? Can you be any of that if you're not?[1]

He convinced me, and as I shared in *The Innovator's Mindset*, "If students leave school less curious than when they started, we have failed them."[2]

---

1   Will Richardson, "Curiosity Is the Cat," Will Richardson—Blog, February 11, 2017, accessed November 10, 2025, https://willrichardson.com/curiosity-is-the-cat/.
2   Couros, *The Innovator's Mindset*.

When students enter school, does "schooling" light that flame of inquisitiveness that kids are predisposed to at a young age (so many questions, all of the time!), or do we extinguish it? This is a question I have pondered for years and am trying my best to address.

Curiosity is not just about our interest in information; it can also lead to a deeper understanding of others, especially those who think differently from us.

CURIOUS OR JUDGMENTAL?

Like many people, I was glued to the finale of *Ted Lasso*, and I loved the warmhearted nature of the show. As much as I enjoyed the ending (no spoilers!), one scene from the show went extremely viral. It stuck with many, not only because of the delivery but because of the much-needed societal lesson it provided.

The character Ted Lasso, amazingly played by *Saturday Night Live* alum Jason Sudeikis, shares a quote he attributes to Walt Whitman that while perhaps famous before the show was made even more so because of the context of the scene it appeared in: "Be curious, not judgmental."

After I rewatched the scene, I leveraged ChatGPT to provide a summary:

> There is a famous scene where Ted challenges Rupert to a game of darts. Rupert assumes Ted is clueless because he underestimates him. But before making his winning throw, Ted tells a story about how he was underestimated his whole life because people never asked questions; they just judged.
>
> The line he delivers is powerful:
>
> "Be curious, not judgmental."
>
> Ted goes on to share that he spent years learning to play darts every Sunday with his father, something nobody bothered to ask. He modelled what it means to stay open,

PRINCIPLE 5

humble, and always learning, even in the face of arrogance and dismissal.³

The same is true when applied to education. Has some of the contentiousness created in the classroom come to reflect a mantra that's the exact opposite of Ted Lasso's phrase? "Be judgmental, not curious" (Please don't quote me on this!) just does not have the same moral ring to it. Yet, this ethos has been an issue in education, whether we want to admit it or not.

I remember in March 2020, for about two weeks, families loved educators as they realized how hard it was to deal with one or a few children throughout the day. They couldn't fathom what that would be like multiplied by ten, twenty, or even thirty. But that feeling wore off, and I did see personal and sometimes even petty attacks on educators.

That year, I literally brought a group of educators together to write the book *Because of a Teacher* to share inspiring stories of educators in our own lives who made a positive difference. It was my way of trying to say thank you to education while many felt the world was saying, "Screw you."

Did that book make a dent and have the impact I had hoped on the morale of the profession? Not even close. But if everyone in the world said, "Why try?" when things are seemingly worse, no impact would be made at all. I believed that it was more important to try and fail than to not try at all.

But if we're being honest, there has been some contentiousness thrown back on families. I am not saying you personally did that as an educator or community leader, but I bet you might have at least seen it.

For example, I've seen some school leadership call parent groups names when challenged. Whether you think the name-calling was warranted or not, my question is, Did it help? Did we model curiosity and

---

3   *Ted Lasso*, season 1, episode 8, "The Diamond Dogs," directed by Declan Lowney, written by Brendan Hunt, aired September 11, 2020, on Apple TV+, 14:22.

ask why people had concerns, or was the field of education made more judgmental in the process?

DISCOMFORT CAUSES GROWTH

Again, I do not see this as the norm in education, but often the loud minority *becomes* the majority's perception of how any group is perceived.

I know it may cause some discomfort to bring this up, but we have said variations of "Discomfort causes growth" in classrooms for as long as I can remember as a student, teacher, and administrator, so the same must be true for adults, right?

And if you think that I'm making this up, unfortunately, as the kids say, I do have the "receipts." I remember seeing a video about annoying parents in education and the following comments posted below the video by people in the profession (who I would never name!).

> STRAIGHT FACTS. Parents shifted the balance. They lowered their expectations for their kids and increased them for teachers. Parents ARE the problem.
>
> If they don't like how teaching is done they can always homeschool and indoctrinate their own kids instead of ruining classrooms
>
> Parents and admin are the problem!

Listen, as both a parent and an educator, I can tell you that I have faltered tremendously in both areas and have done things I regret (many of which I have already shared in this book), but do comments

PRINCIPLE 5

like this bring our community closer together or drive it further apart? Many people in education wear different hats, and I hate to tell you that when I see this, my teacher hat is quickly replaced by my dad hat.

I did not connect names to these comments because we all (including myself, as evidenced by the Dave Burgess story shared earlier) have had moments when we said things online that have affected people for days, weeks, and perhaps longer. We don't think about it again, and sometimes those on the other side never get over it. I judge these comments the way I judge myself: I had a bad moment that I wish I could take back, but it does not define who I am as a person.

But as the *Ted Lasso* scene reminds us, we can bring more people together when we start through a lens of curiosity rather than judgment.

The kids are watching. What do we want them to see?

MODEL THE PROCESS, NOT JUST THE PRODUCT

Before I proceed with the second confession, I want to share that what I wrote above was excruciatingly difficult to write. If you know my work, you know I have done my best to be pro-educator as much as possible, so I am always concerned that when I share things like the above, people think I am the exact opposite of what I am trying to be.

However, being an advocate does mean that sometimes you have to share hard truths, and that is one of them. As I mentioned earlier, I used to tell my staff, "I can't fix problems if I don't know they exist," and this principle is also true in this book.

My hope in sharing what I just did was that it could solve a problem. And pretending a problem doesn't exist will only ensure it becomes worse.

And that is the whole premise of the principle of this chapter: Learn in a way that you would expect from students, as learning leads to growth.

In an effort to show you the process and not just the product, I'll share my second writing confession: I used ChatGPT to help me figure out how to tie in an illustration for this book when I was experiencing writer's block. I'll lift the curtain for you.

In chapter 4, I shared the Van Halen M&M's story and how I love telling it to as many people as possible. I knew that, somehow, I was going to include it in this book.

As any writer would tell you, there are times when writer's block is a thing, and although we may know what we want to say, we may have a hard time articulating it.

I knew the story would be a great fit for building on people's strengths, but I was stuck on how to get there. So I opened ChatGPT, asked if it was familiar with the story (can you imagine if it said, "No, what are you talking about?" Not happening!) and wrote the following prompt: "Is there a way I can connect it to building on people's strengths in an organization?"

Using AI in this manner as a thought partner helped me gather my thoughts and encouraged the writing process. This is not the first book I have ever written, but it is the first book that I have ever written since these tools have existed.

The traditional practice of writing has developed my learning ability in a way I could not have imagined when I first started. It has shown me that some of the most "traditional" things we do in school (reading and writing) will always have a place in learning. It has made me reframe my language to never use the term "traditional teaching" as a negative term. "Traditional" does not equal bad, just as "new" does not equal good.

Yet, connecting the traditional practice of self-reflection with AI can really push our own personal development in a way we expect from students. The two can coexist and make us smarter if we are willing to see and leverage the benefits of each of them.

I could have easily said nothing about how I utilized AI to help me write here, but sometimes showing the process is more important than the product. The hope is that now that you know what I did, you will think, *Hmmm . . . how could I do something similar in my work?* and that will spur further learning.

Going back to the confidence spectrum mentioned earlier in the book, I am comfortable saying, "I was stuck, and here is how I unstuck myself." I am not the smartest person you will meet, but I am a voracious learner.

Sharing that process, and my own discomfort in some of the words I have written in this book, with you is my own version of learning in a way that I would expect from students. It is my way of saying, "Sometimes, this stuff is hard, but through my willingness to try and share how I have learned, I can become better and hopefully inspire others to do the same."

I have no idea what the future entails, but I hope that my own children, and every student in our schools, will have the ability to say, "This is hard, but I will be able to figure it out."

If we want to get them there, they often have to see the road we took, not just the destination. The same is beneficial for our communities.

FROM ADVERSARY TO ADVOCATE

One of the falsehoods that has been perpetuated in education for as long as I can remember is the following: My child's education needs to look similar to my own when I was a kid.

As a dad, I can't tell you how wrong this statement can be.

All parents, including myself, want what's best for their own children. I've worked with schools all over the world, and many of the things I appreciated as a child are still prevalent throughout classrooms. A warm environment, a caring teacher, extracurricular activities that spur a love of sports and the arts. These things were amazing in my childhood, and I still see them in schools all over the world.

What has changed is that there's definitely more of a focus on stoking curiosity and creativity (here come those C words again!) while appreciating the uniqueness of each child, all in those same caring environments I appreciated as a child.

Many things that needed to stay the same did, and some of the things that needed to change followed suit. I have benefited from experiencing that while working within schools and seeing it from the outside looking in. But many families do not have the same access that I do. They do not get to see those incredible experiences kids have, and although it feels like many times they are saying, "I want for my kids what I had as a student," the reality is, "I know no other experience than the one I had as a student, and I turned out just fine."

When you start with the assumption that families want what's best for their children, the onus now shifts to determining how we ensure families see how much better school is today than it was in the past.

My solution to that problem was to invite them into the process. As an administrator, there was not one single professional learning day with my staff that did not include family involvement, and sometimes, depending on their age, students.

We would invite parents to actually partake in professional learning days as equal participants so that they could learn alongside us and see what new things were happening in our schools. Of course, we could not invite all families, simply because we did not have the room, but we would invite different families in each time. Please note, this was not for confidential meetings that involved the privacy of our students and families; it was for professional learning days. If we were going to teach something to our students, we had no issue having parents be part of the process.

But it wasn't that we just invited them in, it was also *who* we invited in. We wanted to ensure that families who were excited about new opportunities for their kids had the chance to be a part of those days as well as the parents who had reservations about the new things we were considering.

PRINCIPLE 5

We knew if we invited people who were making assumptions based on a lack of information, we'd be able to address some of the biggest issues that arise head-on.

This is a consistent issue in education. We often want to tap into those who agree, rather than those who push back. For years, I have watched top academic students (not necessarily the "smartest" students, because some of the smartest kids in our schools struggle academically) being sent to "student voice" conferences, when you would probably get better feedback from those who perhaps aren't the biggest fan of schools, as evidenced by the meme below.

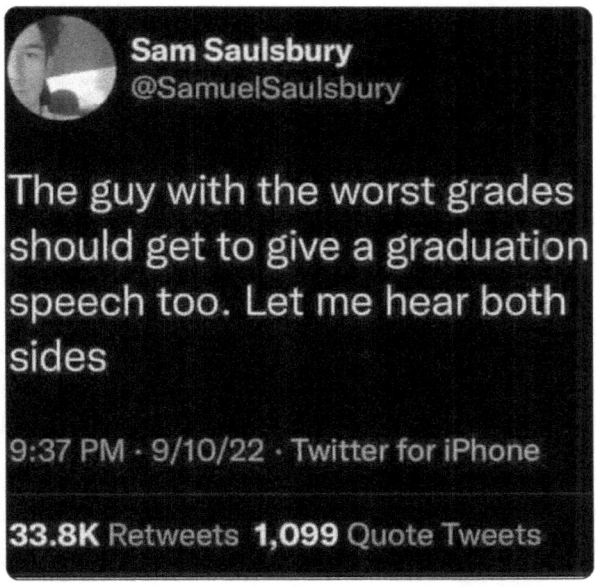

Often, when we brought in the families that weren't sure about, unfamiliar with, or even adversaries of some of the new school initiatives, they had a change of perception once they experienced it with our staff.

LEARNING WITH CURIOSITY

Curiosity is part skepticism and part wonder. We wanted to address families' skepticism without discounting it. Then, based on our own curiosity, we could learn from and leverage their feedback.

It didn't always work out so simply, but I often would ask for feedback and, sometimes, even implement community suggestions—not because I felt pressured to do so, but because they had perspectives that I hadn't considered. What shifted was that not only had they experienced the learning, they, as the community, saw their fingerprints on the implementation of it in the school. They were not going to advocate against something they helped create! (More on this in the next chapter!)

Some of the biggest adversaries of what we were doing in the community were now our biggest advocates.

I cannot remember a time we ever had parents walk out of those sessions and say, "I experienced this, and we need to go back to the way it was when I was a kid!"

Yet several times they did remark, "This is so much better than when I was a kid!" That was the hope of the process! Not only would they experience how much more improved school was from a first-person perspective, but then they would go out and tell the community.

Do you know who parents like listening to? Other parents. The same is true with teachers. They like listening to other teachers. If I see myself in you, I am more likely to listen.

But what is also important is that we weren't trying to manipulate families to buy in to what we were "selling." They took ownership. They became our partners in learning, and personally, it grew me exponentially to be in their presence.

The side benefit of the process of bringing families into the learning process was not only that they became our biggest advocates, but their presence made us better.

PRINCIPLE 5

We weren't trying to be central to the community; we were trying to build community together.

ADDRESS THE PROBLEM BEFORE IT BECOMES ONE

Having led learning on technology and innovation for the majority of my career, my work is inherently rooted in navigating change. But as much as I appreciate learning new things, I also appreciate my routines, and when they are disrupted, I can become irritable—at best.

What I know is what I like, and what I like is what I know. So it's hard to go from what you know. And this is true with all families.

Much of my job is working with families on the opportunities that technology provides. These "parent nights" can be especially daunting when I don't know the families prior to presenting to them. It's much easier to be mean to a stranger you don't agree with when you assume you're likely never to see them again.

One of the things I noticed about these sessions was that no matter how many times I presented, I would often get a parent—or two, or seven—who would bring a notebook, write some stuff down, and seemingly, no matter what I said or addressed, ask questions that were prepared ahead of time based on the description of the session rather than what I'd said. No matter how many times I would adjust and tinker with the presentation, the same questions kept coming up, although I felt I had done my best to address them.

I decided not to just say my points louder but to rethink my approach.

Instead of trying to address the pushback I knew I was going to receive throughout the presentation, I decided to name it right at the beginning.

I would start off with something like this:

> Hey, everyone. My name is George Couros, and I am going to share some things with you on technology in education, from both my perspective as an educator and as a dad.
>
> But before I do that, I want to know that we agree on two things that have helped me shape this presentation. The first one is the following: We want to ensure your kids are safe. Do you agree with me?

Of course, their heads nodded an emphatic yes!

> Great! The second agreement I want to share with you is the following: We want to ensure that your kids have every opportunity to be successful in our world today. Do you agree with me?

Again, emphatic nodding.

The first time I did that, the energy in the room shifted to a much more positive vibe. It was palpable.

So why make those two statements?

Because those two statements were variations of the pushback I was getting every single time, no matter what I said. But instead of dancing around the topic, I named it directly, and, immediately, that room knew I had the same goals in my work that they had for their children.

If I would have been judgmental and not curious, I would have just assumed I knew better. But since I'm trying to model what I expect from students in school, I grew. I found a willingness to learn about and from others.

MOVING FORWARD

In *Innovate Inside the Box*, I shared that it's essential that we embody three types of learning in our leadership:

> Learning for our community

PRINCIPLE 5

Learning about our community
Learning with our community

When you embrace these three areas, you realize that we can get to where we want to go much faster than we could without that support.

But the important side benefit is that the kids see us being who we hope they come to be.

Being curious, not judgmental—as Ted Lasso shared—is more about people than it will ever be about information.

Look for the good in others, and you are way more likely to find it.

It will also help you create a vision together that you could have never done alone.

> ### QUESTIONS FOR DISCUSSION
>
> 1. What does it mean to learn in a way you would expect from your students? What is that expectation you have? How can you define it with your community?
> 2. How can being curious instead of judgmental improve our relationships at school?
> 3. What is one small way you can share more of your learning process with others?

CHAPTER 6

PRINCIPLE 6

CREATE A VISION, TOGETHER

Do you believe kids should learn the "basics" in education?

This is a really important conversation, and many would absolutely say, "Yes! Of course. We need that more than ever!"

If you believe that, great! Here is the next question I have for you, then: What are the basics in our current day?

For most of my life, many would refer to the basics as the three Rs: reading, writing, and arithmetic, which shows whoever made up that idea didn't have the basics down, since only *reading* actually starts with the letter R.

For someone who is really focused on innovation, I do know that foundational skills such as reading and writing are crucial to anything we will do in the future.

One time, someone said to me, "We don't even need spelling tests in our world today! Kids have access to spell check!"

PRINCIPLE 6

My first thought was, *Yeah, but you have to at least be in the vicinity of the word! You can't just slap the keys and hope for the best!*

As I was writing this book, I heard someone share that in today's world, "The number one skill employers are looking for is the ability to leverage AI," and my first thought was, *Not if they can't read and write.*

While reading the book *The AI-Driven Leader* by Geoff Woods (it might shock you, based on the title of the book, what I am about to share), the following resonated: "The idea was simple but incredibly powerful: identify the one thing you could do such that by doing it, everything else would be easier or unnecessary."[1]

It made me think about this answer in the context of education. What would that one thing be that would ensure students are set up for success?

To me, it would be having the ability to read and write.

Of course, other things matter in learning, but the ability to read and write seems foundational to everything. In his book *Hidden Potential*, Adam Grant shares this:

> Basic literacy makes it possible to leverage character skills more effectively—to be proactive in learning more and learning faster. Prosperity rises as people become more capable of absorbing new ideas and filtering out old ones.[2]

But we often make things messy when the answer is a straight line. So if we agree on the importance of reading and writing as skills every child needs to be successful, what are the other basics that are essential?

To this day, many would say cursive handwriting is something every child should be able to do, while many of those same people who can write cursive couldn't figure out how to get on a Zoom call.

---

1 Geoff Woods, *The AI-Driven Leader: Harnessing AI to Make Faster, Smarter Decisions* (AI Thought Leadership, 2024).

2 Adam Grant, *Hidden Potential: The Science of Achieving Greater Things* (Viking, 2023).

While I have heard many criticisms of younger people mocking older generations' inability to use technology, I remember seeing a meme once that said something along the lines of, "The next time you complain about having to show your parents how to use their mobile phone, remember they that had to teach you how to use a spoon!" Fair enough!

In *The Innovator's Mindset*, I kept emphasizing that there's no innovation without basic skills:

> *The* basics are important, but we need to go beyond knowing to creating and doing. Understanding how to read and write doesn't make you a writer. By contrast, if you are a writer, it's a given that you know how to read and write.[3]

Basics are the foundation for the skills that are critical for our success and innovation in today's modern world.

So, what do I think the basic skills or desired outcomes are for learners in your community? Honestly, I have my thoughts, but it is not my place to share them with you. In fact, I pose the question for you to contemplate with your community. Empathize with and understand the current context of your school. Come together with various stakeholders to determine the goals in your community.

Although the question is a starting point, the real power and payoff comes in finding and defining the answers together, not just for the students but even with them.

HELPA, HELPA, HELPA THE KIDS!

I told my kids that I was going to talk about one of their favorite songs and videos in this book, and although I am reluctant to share this due to the lack of widespread familiarity of the band to readers of the book, the kids are extremely excited about this story.

---

3 Couros, *The Innovator's Mindset*.

PRINCIPLE 6

Flight of the Conchords quickly became one of the biggest bands to come out of New Zealand—not based on record sales, but because they have two members, which goes beyond the standard one-person New Zealand band (their joke, not mine).

The two members of the comedy band, Bret McKenzie and Jemaine Clement, have a cult-like following due to their catchy and comedic tunes.

And as funny as I found them, it wasn't until I saw a video of a new single in 2012 that I became fascinated by the duo. "Feel Inside (And Stuff Like That)," the name of the song, doesn't make much sense.[4]

The video opens by revisiting their TV show, with Murray (the band manager) and Bret and Jemaine excited about the possibility of recording a charity song for the Cure Kids organization's Red Nose Day, which is a "much-loved campaign that rallies New Zealanders to support critical research into serious childhood illnesses."[5]

The band decides to do some research on what they should write about, and they interview kids to find out what they are interested in. The interviews with kids—probably ranging in ages from four to nine years old—are some of the most adorable things you will ever see.

The band asks kids what has made them sick before, and a young girl shares how she got sick from eating too much "bubble mixture" because she wanted to turn into a bubble, while another pair of children suggests that the band needs to raise "a million and a hundred, ten and twenty-one dollars" for the charity. I also love when they ask a young girl what rhymes with *better* and she says, "feta," which technically rhymes and it's awesome.

Seriously, watch the video, because I don't want to tell you too much about what the kids say, but it is so absolutely cute.

---

4   "Feel Inside (And Stuff Like That)," YouTube video, 9:50, posted by Flight of the Conchords—Official Cure Kids Long Version, August 27, 2012, https://www.youtube.com/watch?v=py_30jZGUYk.

5   Cure Kids, "Red Nose Day Returns," accessed November 10, 2025, https://www.curekids.org.nz/news/article/red-nose-day-returns.

Feel Inside: FOTC (Video)

The lyrics come from the answers provided by the kids, including the chorus. Although it makes little sense, if you watch the entire video and listen to the song, that chorus will be stuck in your head for days, minimum.

As the interviews end at approximately 10:21, the video starts with an array of singers from New Zealand, across different genres. Bret and Jemaine took all the raw, unfiltered input from the children and turned it into a song that blended humor with genuine heart, welcoming the aspirations of the kids into the final product.

And what happened with the song?

It went straight to number one in New Zealand and raised over $1 million for the charity (probably closer to a million and a hundred and ten and twenty-one dollars) with something that the community, with kids, created together.

The video demonstrates the power of how listening to the voices you serve can create something totally aspirational, even while being a bit messy and overly joyful. It's also a great reminder that when people feel connected to the process, they are more likely to support and champion the result.

SHARED VISION

And do you know why my kids were so excited about me writing about this song and putting it into the book? Because they saw kids being a part of the process and adults coming together to create something beautiful because of their inspiration.

PRINCIPLE 6

In their book, *Lead Like a Pirate*, Beth Houf and Shelley Burgess wrote the following, which has always stuck with me: "People are less likely to tear down a culture that they have helped build."[6]

Building a vision and mission and leading actions together might take longer to do, but our time is better spent in a community building something up than it is fighting to tear something (or even one another) down.

So, what could building a shared vision actually look like in practice?

Superintendent Deidre Roemer is a leader who is beyond aspirational in her thinking and practice. I've witnessed Deidre's leadership firsthand, and she understands the importance of building community first to build a vision together that can last.

When Deidre stepped into her district, she knew that there were great things happening that she could build upon, but she also knew they could go further together.

Prior to her arrival, there had been four superintendents in five years. That kind of turnover doesn't just disrupt leadership, it erodes trust. And when you're new, there is often pressure to come in with the "answer." But Deidre didn't see it that way. She told me:

> During my first few weeks on the job, I got asked over and over again what my vision for the district would be and in what direction I would take us. I repeatedly shared back that it is not something I decide on my own . . . It was essential to set a road map on how we were going to meet shared goals that would bring the community together around our schools and stick, no matter who was in charge.

The word *shared* was not just a placeholder. She meant it. Instead of rushing into change, she started by listening.

---

[6] Shelley Burgess and Beth Houf, *Lead Like a PIRATE: Make School Amazing for Your Students and Staff* (Dave Burgess Consulting, 2017).

Before she officially took the job, she visited schools and spent time learning how things worked. She met with families, staff, students, and members of the school board. What she heard was a mix of pride, frustration, and the strong desire for communication and consistency. And instead of creating a vision on her own, she invited the community to help build one together.

To kick things off, she said, "We needed a diverse group that represented the community, the families, the staff, and the students." Invitations went out to parents, local business owners, teachers, and even students. More than sixty people joined the strategic planning committee, meeting every two weeks throughout the fall and winter.

Deidre shared how the process began:

> We spent some time doing empathy interviews to get to know one another in the first meeting, and then looked at strategic plans from a number of other school districts. Those plans were blown up and posted all over the room. Warm feedback on red sticky notes and cool feedback on blue ones.

And the most important part? She did not write the plan. In her words:

> I facilitated the process and gave input as we went. I could jump in when groups were stuck, and then walk away while they had the discussion. Our mission, vision, values, and goals were developed with feedback from tons of people and are owned by the whole community.

If you build it, they will come. But who will stay?

When the plan was presented to the board for approval, committee members were present to explain the rationale behind the work. The plan passed unanimously. But more importantly, it's now a plan that's been implemented and leveraged.

Deidre discussed how they used the shared plan as a tool to interview and hire, set school improvement plan goals, and build off of a blueprint for principal and teacher goals. They reviewed the plan and let it define their professional learning. She said, "We live and breathe our plan all the time and communicate updates often."

The results were significant. "Parents got to share their hopes for our schools and what they needed from us so we can be partners in figuring it out together," Deidre said.

The staff said they felt the work they were doing mattered. The plan became a steady reference point that created a sense of purpose and direction for the staff and the board.

"When we have a conflict with a team of teachers or a community member on the work we are doing, we use the plan as our anchor," she said. "It clearly outlines our goals and helps people make sense of what we are doing, why we do it, and how we will show evidence of progress."

This is what happens when a vision is not just talked about, but built through a process that includes the people who will carry it forward. It becomes something people are committed to, not because they were told to follow it, but because they were a part of creating it.

MOVING FORWARD

If you think back to the story of "Feel Inside (And Stuff Like That)," the message is clear: When people are part of the process, they are more likely to stay engaged in the progress.

Whether it's students helping to write a song that raises money or a community shaping a vision for a school district, the real power is not just in what is created; it's in how it's created.

New initiatives, referendums, strategic plans, or even redefining the "basics" require us to lean into the most essential leadership skill: listening. When people feel heard, they are more likely to commit. When they help build the direction, they are more likely to walk the path.

As I reflected on what Deidre shared with me, I thought about the famous line from *Field of Dreams*: "If you build it, they will come."

But if you build it alone, they might come. Will they stay? Will they feel ownership? When a community builds something together, the message changes. "If we build it together, they won't just come; they'll stay, contribute, and thrive."

Earlier, I shared the advice Mary Lynne Campbell once gave me: "After you leave a school, ask yourself what your fingerprints will be." My hope is that any fingerprints I leave behind are just one set among many, part of something that was created through shared purpose and made stronger by the people involved.

Build it together. It will not only last longer, it will lift everyone it touches.

> **QUESTIONS FOR DISCUSSION**
>
> 1. What do you believe are the basics students need to thrive in today's world, and how might those differ from the past?
> 2. Why is it important for a school or district vision to be created with the community, rather than by one individual or small group?
> 3. How can we ensure that everyone—students, families, staff, and community members—feels ownership and connection to the direction we are trying to move in together?

PART II
THE PERSPECTIVES

The six principles that I shared in the first part of this book were meant to be pretty straightforward, but if we expected everything to work exactly the way we wanted it to, then we would be discounting the human experience. When someone says, "This method of teaching has worked for 90 percent of students!" my first thought is, *Well, what did you do about the other 10 percent? Did you ignore them and say, "Good enough!" or did you revise and think about how you can adjust what you need to do to get where you want to go?*

The purpose of the principles is that we often make the simple complex, when it should be the other way around. When we deal with the messiness of the human experience, the simpler our ideas, the more we can deal with the complexities of people, which is where your main focus should be—always.

And now, the next part.

The chapters on perspectives aren't about "how to do it right" every time. Things will definitely go wrong. But in the chapters ahead are some stories, ideas, and strategies that might guide you through the messiness or help you start over again the next day.

As a side note, a little trick I've used over the past several years is that when I have a bad day, I go to bed as soon as possible and start all over again. In the same way we encourage teachers to give students a fresh start every day, we have to do that for ourselves.

Because when you are trying to move people forward, together, there will be some bad days. It is inevitable.

In fact, there is a lot to be learned in that messiness, and that is why I will share some moments that I am proud of, some I would take back, and the learning I had along the way. The goal of these chapters isn't to hand you answers. It's to offer a lens, or maybe even a mirror, so you can better make sense of your own context.

Because that's where leadership lives: not just in the big decisions, but in how we see, how we adapt, and how we grow.

Leading by example starts with learning by example, and I hope the next chapter will give you that space to grow. Principles give us direction. Perspectives help us stay grounded along the way.

Let's keep going! We all need you!

CHAPTER 7

PERSPECTIVE 1

WE ARE ALL SOMEBODY'S KID

It's pretty impossible for me to write an entire book without somehow mentioning my love for the sport of basketball. Not only did I play the game as a child and as an adult, but I was also blessed to coach and become a referee, sometimes doing all three roles in the same year.

I appreciate the learning I gained from each role, especially being both a coach and an official. These experiences provided perspectives you might never have if you only stood on one side of the court. It was tough to get mad at an official as a coach because I knew what that role felt like. At the same time, I had patience for coaches because I had been in their shoes too.

The same is true in education. My goal as a principal was to be the administrator I wanted when I was a teacher, not necessarily the principal I actually had, although I was fortunate to learn from several great ones.

It's easier to understand some of the frustrations teachers have with education when you remind yourself what it was like to be in their position. Empathy is crucial to leadership. Although you don't have to have been in the same role as the people you serve, when you have that experience, you should tap into those past perspectives. But nothing replaces taking time to ask questions, listen, and learn from multiple perspectives to see new and better opportunities.

Experience outside the profession can also help you understand the challenges people go through. Reffing at night, exhausted and sweaty, running up and down the court while fans yelled at me, seemed to prepare me for some tough community discussions the next day at school. Sure, someone might be yelling at me, but at least I wasn't (totally) sweaty.

Here's something I noticed that many officials, no matter the sport, have in common with many educators: No matter what decision you make, you seem to be 100 percent wrong to about 50 percent of people. If you change the call, the other 50 percent might be mad at you.

Although the numbers I shared above aren't scientifically based, the emotional perception can feel 100 percent accurate on too many days. But there was one moment from my officiating days that helped me gain perspective not only as an educator, but also as a son and, later, as a dad.

I remember reffing a basketball game in Canada, where hardly anyone seemed to like basketball. There were maybe twelve fans in the stands, and every noise sounded ten times louder because of the empty gym.

Two gentlemen in particular were yelling at me nonstop. In most cases, you just ignore that, but when it is two out of twelve, it feels much more personal.

They were relentless: "You suck!" "Terrible call, ref!" I thought I was actually pretty good! If you want to officiate any sport, you need thick skin, and your attitude has to land somewhere between confidence and

PERSPECTIVE 1

arrogance or you will quickly fall into insecurity, which makes for a much longer game. The same is true in school leadership.

By halftime, I was more frustrated than usual. Maybe I had had a bad day, maybe I was hangry, but tonight, I wasn't going to just let it slide. I looked at my officiating partner and said, "I'm going over to talk to those two guys." He looked at me like it was a terrible idea, but I ignored him and walked up the bleachers.

The two men noticed me coming and looked visibly uncomfortable. Maybe it was because this wasn't something they were used to, or maybe it was my six-foot-four frame, or maybe it was a combination of both.

I got to their seats, sat beside them, and said, "I really appreciate you being here. As a school principal, I hope parents are actively involved in what's happening in our school, and I admire the passion you're showing for your kids. That means everything to me."

Immediately, their worry eased. But I wasn't finished.

"That being said, the thing I'm struggling with right now is how you're talking to me. We really focus on character in our school, and although I'm not perfect, I think about what I'm modeling when kids see me talking to others, especially when I disagree with them."

A little bit of worry returned to their faces.

I continued, "Again, I want to commend you because I can tell you absolutely love your kids. That means a lot. Do you know who else loves their kids? My mom and dad, and they're sitting right behind you right now."

What looked like subtle worry turned into embarrassment and maybe a touch of nausea. Here's the thing, though: My parents were not there. I have no idea why I said that. I walked back to the court as quickly as I could, thinking I'd get busted since nobody in the stands looked over forty.

Do you know what I heard from them in the second half? Nothing.

Although my parents weren't there (they did come to some of my games, and it always looked a little shady when people cheered for the ref), the thought that they might have been there and how those guys were treating me in front of my family gave them pause.

It's worth noting a key aspect of this interaction.

Did you notice the first thing I said when I walked over? I complimented them on their attendance and enthusiasm. Not as sarcasm—but as authentic appreciation. I made sure I wasn't "standing on one side of the court" by recognizing their position and perspective.

Pushing past your own discomfort and meeting people by first recognizing their value is a disarming way to move past contentiousness and build something together.

I've heard many educators complain that parents aren't active in their child's school experience. Here were two dads doing precisely what we say we want more of, even if it wasn't with the demeanor I'd hope for.

To see and acknowledge something good in them when it was incredibly hard to do so broke the tension and opened a pathway to something better.

We are all somebody's kid.

Including those two dads. If I wanted to be treated with respect and dignity, I had to do my best to be what I expected from them.

MOVING FORWARD

When dealing with conflict in your community, you don't have to be a pushover or let anyone degrade you in a way that would embarrass you if the people closest to you were watching.

But when you keep in mind that we are all somebody's kid, you have an opportunity not only to see humanity in the people who seem to be your biggest adversaries but to model what you hope for your own students and children.

PERSPECTIVE 1

> ## *QUESTIONS FOR DISCUSSION*
>
> 1. How can remembering that we are all somebody's kid change the way you approach conflict or criticism?
> 2. Why is it important to recognize and acknowledge something positive in others, even during difficult interactions?
> 3. What experiences have helped you develop empathy for people in roles different from your own?

CHAPTER 8

PERSPECTIVE 2

ELEVATING THROUGH INTENTIONAL LANGUAGE

Writing a book is a challenging process, but choosing a title is something that I will lose sleep over. When the idea behind this book first came to me, surprisingly the title popped into my head immediately.

Here was the first iteration: *DividED: Moving People Forward, Together, in Contentious Times.*

I liked the subtitle, and I knew the single word "DividED" was a nice little play on words while also being provocative.

As a father of three, I have been hopelessly addicted to puns, but just like my craving to continuously do the Hokey Pokey, I turned myself around! (Not my joke, but definitely my kind of joke!)

But that title was just not for me. I want to create something that people aspire toward, not run away from.

Unfortunately, I do know that in education people are drawn to the negative in many aspects. When I have done parent workshops on "Leveraging Technology for Meaningful Learning with Your Children,"

PERSPECTIVE 2

I can have between two and twelve people attend (like a Canadian high school basketball game). Make the "Your Kid Is Likely Going to Be Abducted Online" and you will get a packed house (Canadian hockey game).

Negative language—like focusing on division rather than moving forward, together, in a book title—validates fears, speaks to frustrations, and keeps us in a struggle. When we use intentional, positive language that lifts everyone up, we elevate the people around us to see themselves in the process and play a part in finding solutions.

People are often drawn to the negative, not only in what we want to see, but also in what we want to say.

For example, when do people often leave reviews about a restaurant? Not the nine times that they love the experience but the one time they hate it.

After a professional learning session or asking for staff feedback, do you ever think about how the comments are overwhelmingly positive? Or do you let that one negative review eat away at you for hours, maybe even days?

I have. In fact, I can remember negative reviews of books I have written in the past, such as this blast from the past: "Had to use this book for a class. I got an 'A' in the class, but really did not find this book very helpful in improving my teaching."

They still gave me 2 out of 5 stars though, so I guess it wasn't that bad! Congratulations on your A, random reviewer! Maybe the wrong person is writing the book!

(Five minutes later after reading all the 1 and 2 star reviews . . . Breathe, George!)

Anyway, we are drawn to the negative, and although I know that's true, it doesn't necessarily help bring people together, or move people forward. Can we nudge people in that direction?

For example, I had to go to an emergency dentist because I lost a tooth (unfortunately, not from a Canadian hockey incident, but from eating granola, but that is our secret!), and those places just give me anxiety.

They knew I was scared, were very comforting, and, as painlessly as possible, extracted my tooth. I remember going up to the counter and saying, "I just want to let you know that I hate dentists, and you, you weren't horrible. That is about as nice as I have the ability to be in this situation I didn't want to be in!" She laughed because she knew I was joking (kind of), and pointed to a sign on the desk with a QR code to Google Reviews and the number of five-star ratings the business had received. She encouraged me to provide my own feedback, to which I obliged immediately. I wouldn't go there for a holiday, but I might come back if I lose another round with a rogue piece of granola.

This made me think about how schools should incorporate something similar. As someone who works with schools all over the world, but mostly in North America, I often rent a vehicle and, to find where I am heading, open up Google Maps, which includes "reviews" of the school.

If I based my belief on what those schools were like on their reviews, I would be terrified to go. However, having worked in schools myself and with them, I know that those reviews are not an overall reflection of the school but rather the dominant narrative of those who are upset with the school in the moment. One time, I suggested a school do something similar to the dentist's office and ask for reviews based on positive experiences. The leader said, "Well, our community knows our school is good, so we don't really need to worry about what it says online." That might be true, but what about someone new to your community? Would they use the same standard that they use for buying a product on Amazon? Anything with a rating of four or less on Amazon is a no-go for me, and that's for a deodorant or a supplement—not a place where my kids will spend a third of their day!

It's crucial to clarify what I am saying: I am not asking anyone to encourage people to lie about their school, but rather to ensure

PERSPECTIVE 2

that they share the truth when it is positive, because that often takes some coaxing!

When we celebrate the good, it is more likely we look for it and create more goodness in our communities.

This is also why you will never hear me talk about things like antibullying. I have zero interest in telling people what *not* to do. Rather, we should model a focus on leadership and raise the bar for the behaviors we want to see.

My good friend Michelle Baldwin shared with me a subtle anecdote related to this. First, she said to me, "Don't think of an elephant." Then she asked what I thought of first. I can tell you it wasn't Bambi. You get it. I have learned this lesson more times than I can count.

Years ago, speaking at a school in Sydney, Australia, I shared a sentiment I had probably talked about hundreds of times prior. I mentioned that we had teachers in the profession for more than thirty years who were stuck in their ways, teachers who were newer to the job who were trying innovative practices, and vice versa. This has nothing to do with skillset and everything to do with mindset.

The "vice versa" was important in that sentence. I wanted to ensure that no one felt I was saying that younger was better than older, which, honestly, is a common narrative in education.

A few hours later, I received an email from a teacher named "Dorothy," a veteran of fifty-plus years in the profession. She commended me on the extraordinary session but did mention that my singular statement felt like (not kidding) "granny bashing," and I should reconsider my language. She said it somewhat in jest, closed with some kind words, and wished me the best.

She "compliment sandwiched" me, hard. And she made me rethink what I said. Ever since then, I have reversed the order of that statement, and I think of Dorothy when I say something similar to the following: "We have new teachers in the profession who often teach the way they were taught because that was their experience in school and veteran teachers implementing innovative practices, and vice versa. As you all know, age is not the barrier, but it is our mindset."

Dorothy knew that with a subtle shift in thinking I could bring more people in than push people away. You could easily argue that I am now pointing to new teachers and maybe that has some validity, but I rarely hear that our new teachers aren't the ones being innovative while many argue that we are being held back by our more experienced staff.

And it wasn't just the language in that specific sentiment that changed.

You have probably heard sentiments like this (not from me): "AI will not replace you, but a teacher using AI will replace you!" Basically, if you don't use AI, you are out of here, sucker!

Here is a variation that I think better describes the role of the educator and technology: Technology will never replace great teachers, but technology in the hands of a great teacher can be transformational.

A subtle notion in the statement is that you can be a great teacher without the use of technology, but if you use it in a meaningful way, you might even excel your current practice and have more of a meaningful impact on learners.

I know it's subtle, but I'm trying to point out where we can go rather than what we should run from. Once Dorothy pointed out this subtle distinction to me, I started to notice it everywhere.

At a technology conference, one of the presenters said, "We need to de-emphasize memorization," which I am sure I've said some variation of myself. Is the statement wrong? Probably not. Is it helpful? Also probably not. Here is why: Let's say half of the audience in front of you agrees with this statement. By default, that means the other half disagrees. Does that statement bring people closer together or drive them apart? My take is the latter.

So, instead of focusing on the idea that we should de-emphasize memorization, which may push people apart, how do we bring people together while, perhaps, moving them forward? My own language has shifted from focusing on eliminating memorization to inviting people to embrace the idea that progress and success happens when learners develop a deep understanding of the information presented to them. For example, if you memorize something, it doesn't mean you understand it. But if you understand a concept, by default, you will likely remember it. The people who believe that we should de-emphasize memorization are validated and perhaps challenged to consider that knowing basic information is crucial in our pursuit of developing wisdom.

The people who believe memorization is crucial lose nothing but are very unlikely to disagree with the idea that deep understanding is essential.

Through subtle phrasing shifts, you bring people together and forward.

MOVING FORWARD

In recent years, I have seen schools embracing the idea of a "Profile of a Graduate," sharing their aspirations and focus on helping students develop specific skills and attributes that will benefit them into adulthood. But more school communities are shifting that language to a "Profile of a Learner" to embrace the idea that these characteristics are not only helpful to students but also to the community as a whole.

It is often said that one of the best ways we can demonstrate our ability to learn is to change our minds, especially when new information is available. If we want our students to grow in their learning, they have to see it reflected in the adults.

Instead of focusing on what people will lose with any new changes or opportunities, shift the language to what they have to gain.

This idea has been a significant shift for me, and when we use language that signifies an abundance of possibilities, more people are likely to embrace new opportunities.

Considering all of this, if this chapter inspired you, please feel free to leave a review on Amazon. If it didn't, I'm sorry someone made you read it for your class.

QUESTIONS FOR DISCUSSION

1. How does the language we use, especially as educators or leaders, influence whether people feel included or pushed away? Can you share an example where a small change in words had a big impact?
2. Why do you think people often respond more strongly to negative messaging than to positive? What are some ways we can focus on the good while still addressing challenges honestly?
3. Can you recall a time when feedback helped you rethink something important? What did you change, and how did it affect your approach going forward?

CHAPTER 9

PERSPECTIVE 3

LISTEN TO LEAD

As I shared in the last chapter, the language we use to help people see new possibilities is paramount to creating the change we want to see. But as much as what we say and how we say it matter, sometimes saying nothing is the best way to bring people together (says the guy currently writing a book).

Too often in my career, I have spent my time and energy trying to convince people of ways they could move forward and why it mattered so much that they did. I would think of every angle and argument that would prove my point, and I would end up extremely frustrated that no matter what I said, whomever I was talking to seemed to stay exactly where they were when I started. Sometimes they even seemed to move backward to prove a point.

A sentiment I often share with others is that in leadership, our role is to help people move from *their* point A to *their* point B.

I still believe this, but how do you do that if you have no idea what their point A is when you begin? That starts with listening.

And not just listening, but listening with the intent of learning and also an understanding that you can move forward as well.

WHAT DO YOU WANT TO LEARN?

Working at the central office with a school district, I wanted to be as visible as possible in our schools. Being in classrooms and working directly with the staff was a great way to be seen in the spaces I needed to be while also helping me be informed of how I could best help communities.

To this day, my belief remains that central office teams should do as much as possible to remove barriers that prevent schools from performing the most critical work that needs to be done. Too often, the perception from schools regarding district office staff is that they do the exact opposite.

Teachers often share with me that they become nervous and even frustrated when what they see as the "superintendent entourage" teams of three to thirty people walk around classrooms. When there is not a clear goal or transparent feedback, it can be perceived that board members and central office administrators are there more for PR than support and moving forward together.

I hated it when that happened to me; however, I still wanted to be present in schools and help in any way I could. It's why I met one-on-one with the staff—like Suzie, who learned to embrace Instagram for a class project. I made sure they had the space to be heard, and I gave them room to ask me for help in any area they needed assistance with, especially in my focus area of innovation.

Before coming to a school, I would talk to the principal and ask for permission to do so (no one ever said no), and then I would book a substitute teacher or two, who would cover classes for the teachers who would talk with me.

If the teachers were interested in taking an hour with me, they did not have to send me anything ahead of time. I wanted them to have

PERSPECTIVE 3

no prep for our time, but I also knew that even if you have someone cover your class, as a teacher, you still have to do work for the substitute teacher time.

The staff were always excited because they knew I was coming in with no agenda other than helping them in a way that made the most sense to them. It was a great way to identify each person's "point A" through our conversations.

Those one-on-one times would vary wildly in what they looked like and the range of abilities of the adults. We would share niceties, and then I would simply ask them what they would want to learn. There was only one common theme I noticed in every individual session: They all wanted to get better. That is why they were there.

Because I had spent a significant amount of time traveling around the district, I knew most staff members to varying degrees, and there was one time I was shocked by one of the teachers who had booked a session with me. For the sake of this book, we will call her Suzie, and she seemed to be anti-everything at most, and perhaps, anti-George at least. She did not seem to like me or what my role represented, and I felt it every time I entered the school.

My initial assumption was that she booked the time to yell at me, and I was okay with that because at least we would be talking. My Greek family had prepared me for moments like this all my life. Our dinners as a child would have made Jerry Springer blush, but that was just how our family "talked."

Still, I assumed positive intent. I knew she wanted to learn, regardless of how it appeared. I was there for it! Showing up was a fantastic first step.

Suzie walked into the room, and I welcomed her. Little in the way of pleasantries were returned my way. As she sat down, I asked her what she wanted to learn, and I recall her saying, "Twitter, I guess."

I asked her, "Why would you want to learn Twitter?" Her response was that everyone else was using it (oh, the 2010s!), so she figured she should as well.

It was then that I steered the conversation in a different direction. "I don't want you to learn something because everyone else is using it. I'd like to help you with something you'd like to do. For example, what are you doing in science class right now?"

She lit up a little bit and said, "We are actually doing plant growth right now, and students are drawing what they see and writing observations in their journals."

Enthusiastically, I said, "Suzie, I love this! It sounds great. Can I maybe suggest something to extend that learning?"

Suzie nodded, and I said, "What if we created a classroom Instagram account that you would totally control and have students take pictures of the plant growth. They can document it in the captions while sharing it with families?"

I could tell her interest was piqued, and so I was doing everything to not bust out of my chair with giddiness. She said, "Okay, I will try it, but I don't want any student to show their faces on the page."

At the time, our district had every student, including those in her class, sign waivers that allowed their information to be posted on school accounts. What I could have done was say, "You don't have to worry about that! All the students have waivers signed!"

But I knew better, and I said, "No problem at all!"

This is so imperative to share: In this particular situation, I, along with many others, were ahead of Suzie in our thinking and practice. I could have made her feel bad for not being where we were and tried to push her to *my* point B. But if I did that, she might not only have rejected something new but also decided to take several more steps away.

Instead of complaining that she wasn't moving far enough, I celebrated that she was moving ahead. That is the goal.

As a side note, whatever you think or whatever initiative that you advocate for in your own school community right now is probably something you weren't excited about at some point in your life. People had patience for you (and me), so we exhibit that same patience for others.

PERSPECTIVE 3

Suzie's classroom Instagram page started posting more frequently, and families were so excited to see what their kids were doing in class. They were also making more and more comments, to which the students were replying.

But then I saw a kid's face posted on the account, and my first thought was, *Uh oh . . . this kid is going to be in huge trouble!*

I sat back and noticed that other pictures were being posted, and then I realized she knew what was going on with the account and was totally okay with it.

But I did call her to double-check. I asked her if everything was okay, because I noticed a student had posted a picture on Instagram and I knew she didn't want that.

Suzie replied, "Oh no! Totally fine! Her mom called and asked if she could see her child's face, and since all of the forms were signed, I had no problem with it!"

What unfolded next was that because one parent saw another child posted, she asked if she could see her child as well. Then another and another and, eventually, a group picture at the end of the project, with Suzie beaming with pride and joy!

Through this one-on-one process, Suzie developed *confidence* in trying something new and *gained competence* as she became more comfortable with her learning to the point where she was bragging to others on the staff about her class project.

As she beamed with pride, others pulled me aside and asked me, "How did you get Suzie to do this?" In reality, I just asked her what she wanted to learn and listened.

Not only did she look great in the process, but word spread how valuable that time with me could become, as I was always tailoring it to whatever the individual wanted.

Atul Gawande said, "Interaction is the key force in overcoming resistance and speeding change."[1]

---

1 Atul Gawande, "Slow Ideas: Some Innovations Spread Fast. How Do You Speed the Ones That Don't?," *New Yorker*, July 29, 2013.

Listening and learning from people, even one at a time, can be one of the fastest ways to move your entire organization forward.

MOVING FORWARD

I would love to say that the interaction with Suzie was the norm and everyone was that easy, but then I would be lying to you.

In challenging circumstances, I have learned to step back. When trying to convince someone to try something new, I talk to them and subtly get them to convince me why they shouldn't. And sometimes they are right, and I am wrong. At least in that moment.

Listening is not about manipulating someone's words against them to get them to do what you want them to do. It's about finding common ground so that both parties can move forward.

Listening is helpful to both parties. Maybe you are wrong, and they have valid points. Perhaps you are on the right track, but you find some common ground that you can build on. Or maybe you figure out that neither party will move and that you are better off if you don't spend your time spinning your wheels in the same spot. This is not about proving who's right and who's wrong but finding places to work together to help improve education for all learners.

The next time you feel the need to convince someone of your position, start asking questions and give the person a chance to persuade you of their position. If we are all about learning and growth, this will only benefit our own development.

Want to convince someone to try something new? Stop convincing and start listening. That is the only way you can find out where they are—their point A.

PERSPECTIVE 3

QUESTIONS FOR DISCUSSION

1. What does it mean to truly listen as a leader, and how can that impact the way people respond to change?
2. Think of a time when someone met you at your point A. What did they do that made you feel supported, and how can you replicate that for others?
3. How can we create more opportunities in our schools or organizations for agenda-free one-on-one conversations that build trust and spark growth?

CHAPTER 10

PERSPECTIVE 4

SOMEBODY HATES YOU

How is that for a chapter title?

It might be blunt, but it is true. In fact, it might be the truest thing I say in the entire book. No matter your role, someone in your community probably hates you, and it might even be justified! Some of you might be being forced to read this book for an educational-leadership class right now, and you probably hate me!

People can hate you for not living up to what they think you should be in the role, and sometimes they will hate you for being good at your job. Either way, someone hates you. (But I love you for reading this far even if you hate me! Only love can conquer hate, my friend!)

I am not immune to this either.

There is one staff member in particular who would visibly cringe whenever I spoke, and I swore, if I said her name, she would change it just so she wouldn't have to agree with me, even for a second. She wasn't my favorite person ever either, but as I look back and think about how much I struggled with her, I realize I am at an age where I have the ability to laugh at this more than be upset.

But you don't always feel that in the moment.

PERSPECTIVE 4

IT ONLY TAKES ONE

There was a moment in my speaking and consulting career that I will never forget. It was so awkward and awful at the time, and if you took me back to the theater where it happened, I could point to where the person was sitting and describe them meticulously for a police sketch artist.

I promise you that all of the people that were there will remember this interaction as well.

Before the incident happened, in a room full of 1,500 staff members, I told a story I share often about a student named Kyle who, in my grade-nine math class, thought it would be funny to address me by my first name as a sign of disrespect. When we had a conversation outside the classroom, I shared that he was more than welcome to address me by my first name—upon graduation and turning eighteen years old. Leaving that school and district at the end of the year, I received a message from Kyle on Facebook at 12:03 a.m. that started with, "Hi, George! This is Kyle, George!" This was followed by approximately fifty more uses of the word George in the next hundred words. It has always made me smile. Only seconds after I responded to him, he responded with a "See you, George." I was never to hear from him again.

The point of the story, other than the humorous interaction, is to remind educators that no matter what you say to a student, or even a colleague or community member, they can remember it long afterward. The audience appreciated the reminder.

Later, as shared earlier in this book, I asked the audience for their questions, ideas, and challenges. One person seemed rather enthusiastic to challenge me (which is often the case), but some of the comments felt a bit more personal and not on the topic at hand. As much as I encourage people to challenge my thinking, I am comfortable pushing back if I don't agree, although I try my best to do it in a respectful manner. But I could sense this was turning into more of a personal issue than anything.

As I was trying to wind down the conversation, she wanted to add one last bit to the end of the conversation.

"You know that kid Kyle who sent you that message? Do you know what he was saying?" She paused, looked directly at me, and, from her seat, lunged forward and said, "He was saying, 'F*** YOU.' That is what he was saying. 'F*** YOU!'"

First of all, she wasn't saying the letter F in isolation. I am not comfortable writing out the entire word, but she said every one of those four letters in that word as if they had their own syllable, and she made sure to make distinct eye contact with me while doing so.

There was an uncomfortable silence in the room, as everyone knew she was using the story not to share what she thought Kyle was implicitly saying to me in that message but as a vehicle to share her own thoughts toward me. This way, no one could accuse her of saying something so nasty to me directly and she could say, "Not at all! I was just saying what I thought the student was implying to him!"

Classic high school move—just one that usually comes from a student.

All eyes were pointed toward me. I was a guest in this space. I had no role in the district and no authority. I was a little dismayed that no superintendent did anything, but you could also feel a sense of shock.

I calmly collected myself and said, "Do you know what? Maybe he was saying that. I've had students hate me before, and I'm sure you have too. But, I couldn't tell you what he meant. It was just meant to be a perspective I wanted to share with you all on how our words carry weight." I continued, "What I do feel is that you and I obviously have differences in our beliefs, and I know this conversation is not going in a positive direction, so I am going to turn my attention to others in this room who are eager to learn."

What happened next floored me. The whole room started clapping for my response. Not because I didn't lose my cool, but because I gave her no time to continue.

PERSPECTIVE 4

This story now seems kind of funny, and I have to admit to being impressed. I mean, wow, she had some guts to do that! But she probably had the wherewithal to do it because she had gotten away with it before.

It came as no surprise when I learned afterward that this kind of behavior was not a one-time thing for this staff member. But typically what would happen was that the moment would take over the entire session, and I hadn't been interested in continuing with it at all.

What the staff appreciated was that I didn't get caught up in her interaction but that I shifted my attention to the room and what they wanted to learn. I also demonstrated a sense of character when it was hard to do so.

Even if I did pee my pants a little.

I still tell the Kyle story, and I think of her every time I do. I am confident enough to understand that he might not have had the best intentions or memory of me, but the moral is not that I was a good teacher. It's that our words stick with the people we're talking to and anyone else who's listening.

The audience in that room heard what the staff member said (I think the school district across the way also heard it at the same time), but they also heard my response, or lack thereof. My attention turned to the majority of people who wanted to be heard and supported. If we let everyone who hated us or strongly disliked what we had to say stand in the way of our efforts to build community and move people forward, we would all be frustrated and stuck.

MOVING FORWARD

You often hear, or even say, "We spend 80 percent of our time on 20 percent of our people," referring to many of the issues we face in our school. I have a better formula, though: You should spend 80 percent of your time on 80 percent of your people. These are people who want to learn, grow, and crave mentorship.

What do we often do to that 80 percent? Ignore them or sometimes even punish them by adding more work to their plates because we know they are likely to say yes with a smile while slowly pushing them to burnout for doing a good job.

So what about the 20 percent? You don't ignore them, but the more you build up the 80 percent, the more they will take care of the 20 percent. They will either make them better and correct them when they have to, or, sometimes, they might even push them out. And that is okay sometimes!

People should not stick in jobs where they are miserable. As the saying goes, what you permit, you promote. But what you promote shifts the responsibility to focus on what "we permit" as a community. Elevate the 80 percent, and it will get closer to 100 percent.

QUESTIONS FOR DISCUSSION

1. How can leaders stay grounded and focused when facing criticism or personal attacks, especially in public settings?
2. Why is it important to invest most of your energy into the people who are eager to grow, and how can that influence the culture of your school or organization?
3. Think about a time when someone challenged you in a negative way. How did you respond, and what might you do differently now based on this chapter?

CHAPTER 11

PERSPECTIVE 5

DON'T GET USED TO THE SMELL

In the last chapter, I talked about focusing on the needs of the 80 percent instead of the 20 percent, and although I am not backing away from the sentiment, there is one caveat I need to add.

Sometimes, you are in the 20 percent. Not in a bad way. Perhaps you're the opposite of what you perceive has been holding you back in the past.

Strangely enough, sometimes a school community you are a part of might not be ready for you. It's always better when they know that before you're hired.

DON'T DIM YOUR LIGHT

Early in my teaching career, I was eager to find a job teaching closer to where I was commuting from, and I was excited to apply for an opportunity that seemed to be tailor-made for my skillset and experience at the time. It was the role of an educational technology lead at a school, and it was work that I had vast experience with, so I enthusiastically applied. Upon receiving a request to interview, I remember eagerly preparing for the day.

Then it came, and, I will tell you, it went better than I could have expected. I could tell from the feedback that the administrative team was authentically impressed. I felt that this job was going to happen and it could be a great new start for my career.

Then the superintendent called me and said that although my interview was excellent and I was considered the best interview they had conducted, they were not offering me the job.

Of course, I was confused and asked for feedback on why I wasn't getting the job if they felt I was the strongest interviewee.

I will never forget what they said: "Honestly, your ability in this area is beyond what our staff is doing now, and you will probably scare them." This felt like an "It's not you, it's me" moment, and I never understood it. Honestly, it bothered me tremendously.

In retrospect, I know that some of the best opportunities I have ever had in my life came from *not* getting jobs that I wanted. My career went in a totally different direction, and eventually I became a school principal, which was not something I had ever considered doing.

In that role, our school was considering taking on an initiative that I thought would be a fantastic opportunity for our staff and students. I loved it and took the staff to visit a school that had already implemented what we were considering. Although we thought the program was beneficial to that school, we had a long conversation on our way back to our own school about how, at this time, it wasn't a good fit for where we were.

It wasn't the program; it was us. Now, things started making sense.

There are two reasons I wanted to share this perspective: For those of you who might not have received a job or opportunity that you really wanted, it might not have been because you weren't the top candidate, but you might not have been the right fit.

Does that feel good to hear? Probably not. Here's the deal: If you weren't the best candidate, the solution is to work harder. If you were the best candidate, the solution is the same.

The second reason I wanted to share this is for those who hire. The best "person" isn't always the best fit for your organization or culture.

When I was hired by my favorite leader ever, Kelly Wilkins, the job post was for a "middle school teacher." That was it. They wanted to open the pool for the best fit for their school, not a specific role, as they knew that would limit the candidate pool. In the interviews, they looked at what the person could bring to the school and what they needed. They could move things around if they felt the person was a great fit.

Think of it this way: Getting the best possible people for your organization is way more challenging than switching people around who are already there (but only if the move suits their strengths and passions!).

Luckily, I was the "fit" they found for Kelly's school, and I cannot tell you how much I learned from that experience. It was also a much better opportunity than the one I had lost the previous year.

The best person for the job and the best person for the culture are not always the same. Whether you are applying or hiring, I hope you keep that in mind. We aim to set up the new hire for success as well as the existing team members.

Looking back, I am grateful that the superintendent had the foresight not to put me—or his team—in a situation that would have probably led to more contentiousness than harmony.

But sometimes that foresight isn't always there.

DON'T GET USED TO THE SMELL

As I shared earlier, maybe you are in the 20 percent of people in your organization (or even less) that wants things to improve. Or maybe you just have a different vision for education.

This is probably not the typical advice you would get in an education book, but sometimes you have to step back, evaluate, and decide that you need to go. If you aren't growing, you might need to get going. Sometimes, removing yourself from the picture or situation is the shake-up others need to move forward.

This is a perspective I learned before I was in the field of education.

Anyone who knows me at all would be shocked that I have worked in fields like construction before, because I am not terribly good with my hands. (I actually shot a nail into my hand at one job, but that is a story for another book!)

But after I graduated from high school, I struggled to find a job.

I went to a local recruitment center to help find temporary positions. The first one they offered me was at a pig farm. Even when the recruiting officer was describing the job, she didn't seem too enthusiastic about what she was sharing. There was a highly contagious virus at the farm, so they had to remove all of the pigs (I don't want to think about what that meant!) and clean out the "stuff" from the barn that was carrying the disease.

I was desperate for a job, so I reluctantly accepted. She was shocked, but she told me where to go at night because it was a 24/7 job that required two different shifts.

I remember pulling up outside the barn, and the smell was terrible. So bad. There are no words that could explain how bad it was, only GIFs, but since this is a book, I will let your imagination run wild.

So, so, so bad.

Then I went inside. And the smell went to another level. It was horrendous. I had never smelled anything so bad.

For the next twelve hours, I stood in plastic coveralls with a hose and sprayed the "stuff" from the barn into a grated hole. I was literally up to my knees in it, which was horrible. They fortunately allowed me to bring a Walkman (yes, I am that old) to listen to, since it was an extremely monotonous job, which was the least of my concerns.

PERSPECTIVE 5

But as the hours ticked by, I became used to the smell. What was horrible before eventually just *was*, and I made it through the entire night.

I remember cleaning myself up, walking outside of the barn to my car, and opening the door to what seemed to be the freshest air I had ever smelled in my life. It immediately hit me that what I had thought was horrible before did not seem so bad now.

The next day, I called the recruitment center and told them I couldn't continue. The officer congratulated me for making it longer than others—most hadn't completed a shift. Bless anyone who could do that job because, obviously, it was something that had to be done.

That experience shaped my thinking in how I approach the opportunities I pursue or continue with in my life.

Not because of the job but because of the smell. It was horrible, but, eventually, I got used to it. Until I stepped outside. There have been jobs in my life that I knew were bad for me, but I took them and got used to the terrible situation, and I no longer paid attention. I let bosses speak down to or mistreat me because I felt I had no other options.

But then you walk outside and realize the inside is worse. You just got used to the smell. Here is a little piece of advice I offer you that will only apply to some who are currently reading this: Some of the best things that have happened to me in my career weren't jobs I received but jobs I left. Never stay in a place that doesn't make you feel valued.

I'm sure you've seen this before, but there was a popular meme that went around the internet that I think provides some great advice:

> A bottle of water at Costco is $0.25.
> The same bottle in the supermarket is worth about $0.50.
> The same bottle in a bar costs $2.
> In a good restaurant or hotel, it can be worth up to $3.
> At an airport or on a plane, you may be charged $5.

The bottle and the brand is the same, the only thing that changes is the place. Each place gives a different value to the same product.

When you feel like you are worth nothing and everyone around you belittles you, change places, do not stay there.

Have the courage to change places and go to a place where you are given the value you deserve. Surround yourself with people who really appreciate your worth.

Now, I have not confirmed the prices of water at these separate places (although the meme has inspired me to go to Costco more), but you get the point.

Sometimes, you have to step outside and ask yourself, "Am I in the right place?"

If not, don't get used to the smell. Because if you do, it will be all over you when you walk out of that place, and it will take much longer than you realize to remove it from yourself.

MOVING FORWARD

You can't fix every place, and sometimes, you just aren't a good fit. Many educators have shared with me reasons they've had for staying somewhere. For example, "But these students here need me!" I get it. And they do.

But so do other schools, communities, and organizations. If you lose yourself in giving to others who do not want to receive your gifts, there will be very little you can do for anyone else.

In the moment, you might feel like a failure for not achieving what you had hoped, but changing directions is not the same as quitting. You can't help someone who doesn't want your help. That is a reality.

When things feel bad, you have to stop and wonder if it is just for a moment or if it is an all-the-time thing. Often, the former feels like the latter, but when you step back, you realize it isn't.

PERSPECTIVE 5

Don't dim your light because someone else isn't ready for you.

Keep going. And whatever you do, don't become something you are not that doesn't align with your belief system. You might get the job or opportunity you want, but the cost to yourself will never be worth it.

> **QUESTIONS FOR DISCUSSION**
>
> 1. Have you ever been in a situation where you felt undervalued or out of place? How did you respond, and what did you learn from it?
> 2. What does it mean to be the "right fit" for a team or organization, and how can both leaders and individuals recognize when it's not working?
> 3. How can we create environments where people are encouraged to shine instead of feeling pressured to dim their light?

CHAPTER 12

PERSPECTIVE 6

LEARN TO CLAP FOR YOURSELF

What advice would you give to yourself if you were talking to yourself as a friend?

This is something I always reflect on when I am struggling with things, and ironically, it is hard to take in. We are often our harshest critics and can be our own worst cheerleaders. That being said, I still do my best to step outside of myself and talk to myself like I would a friend.

In the last chapter, I shared how sometimes you just have to know when it's time to move on. In the moment, you might feel like a failure for not achieving what you had wanted.

But when things feel bad, you have to stop and think if this is a "moment" or is this "all the time"?" Often, the former feels like the latter, but when you step back, you realize it isn't. One thing I have learned about tough situations over the years is to never take criticism too harshly.

PERSPECTIVE 6

As I have gotten older, memes like this might make me even laugh about it:

It is way better to laugh at your own shortcomings and missteps than to let someone else do it for you!

But as much as we want to scream out, "Haters gonna hate, and ain'ters gonna ain't!" (shoutout to the movie *The Interview* for that gem!), we also have to learn something else. Don't get too caught up in the compliments either.

As much as we want to feel appreciated for the tireless work we do in education and some of the battles we have won and continue to fight, if you base everything on what someone else says about you—good or bad—you will be constantly seeking validation.

Speaker Les Brown shared, "Sometimes the nicest things you will hear in a day are the things you say to yourself," and there is validity to this, no matter the profession.[1]

---

[1] Les Brown, quoted on the Les Brown Official Website, "Sometimes the nicest things you will hear in a day are the things you say to yourself," accessed November 10, 2025, https://lesbrown.com/.

We have to admit that although students can be challenging, adults come with their own challenges as well (myself included).

But, as University of Texas psychology professor Kristin Neff, author of *Self-Compassion: The Proven Power of Being Kind to Yourself*, told KQED, self-compassion, not self-esteem, is an important trait for getting us through obstacles in our lives:

> Self-esteem is a judgment about how valuable I am: very valuable, not so good, not valuable at all. In contrast, self-compassion isn't about self-evaluation at all. It's about being kind to oneself.
>
> Self-compassion is a healthy source of self-worth because it's not contingent and it's unconditional. It's much more stable over time because it's not dependent on external markers of success such as grades.[2]

The idea of compassion has been prevalent throughout the pages of this book. When things seem to be a struggle with others in your community, no matter their role, it's crucial to moving forward to try and take a step back and understand their point of view and experience.

But if you can do that for others, you have to be able to do it for yourself. You also have to learn to recognize that although you might not be at the point you want to be in your own work, you are probably further today than you had hoped in the past. The only way you can recognize that is if you learn to have gratitude for your own growth.

CLAP FOR YOURSELF

When I was teaching at the high school level, our staff meetings often started with moments of recognition. I knew that I was valued as a staff

---

2 Kristin Neff, interview by Katrina Schwartz, "How Self-Compassion Supports Academic Motivation and Emotional Wellness," KQED MindShift, January 14, 2019, https://www.kqed.org/mindshift/52854/how-self-compassion-supports-academic-motivation-and-emotional-wellness.

PERSPECTIVE 6

member for my contributions to the school, but I never seemed to get that moment in the spotlight at the beginning of those meetings. I will admit that it bothered me, but I knew I wasn't the only one who hadn't had that moment.

Then one meeting started, and I was recognized for something that I had done to help out in the community. I will admit that I can't remember what it was, but I do remember being ecstatic getting that public acknowledgment. I was struggling at this point in my career, and I needed a bit of a lift.

The funny thing is that sometimes these moments are awkward in staff meetings because we don't really know what to do as passive participants. Sometimes we are appreciative of others, sometimes a bit jealous, and, other times, both at the same time—or neither. Depends on the mood!

So as the principal finished with the recognition, I beamed with delight, but everyone else looked a little quiet. Admittedly, this was the first thing on the agenda that morning, so people were still waking up.

During this sort of "stunned silence" in the room, I remember putting my hands under the table, where no one could see them, and starting a light round of applause. Immediately, it had a snowball effect, and everyone started clapping and thanking me for my work, to which I cajoled them with "Aww . . . stop! You don't have to say that!"

My work bestie saw what I had done and started laughing, because he knew the applause was started by me, and everyone else started laughing as they figured it out.

It was meant to provide some humor at the start of the meeting, but as I reflect on that moment, I think about the symbolism of it in my life.

If you're focused on making others happy and doing what they want, they might appreciate you in the moment, but what happens when you say the thing they don't want to hear? This is becoming more prevalent in society as influencers find trending topics and focus more on saying what they think will go viral rather than what would help most. It has also caused some of the contentiousness in the field of education (along with many others), as many look to "rage bait" and get people riled up at others rather than think about how we can find solutions and bring people together.

Divisiveness is trendy. I am just not interested in participating.

So learning to clap for yourself is not about doing what you think others will want you to do. It's about doing what you can to make yourself and the world around you better.

As I said earlier, we should never get too caught up in the criticism or the compliments of others, but we should acknowledge when we need growth or celebration in our own lives.

Others might not give you the credit you feel you deserve, but you go home with you. If you do what you know is right by yourself and others, applause will be in your future—it just might be only coming from one source.

But that one source can snowball into appreciation from others.

MOVING FORWARD

In the Marc and Angel blog post "10 Hard Things You Shouldn't Be Afraid to Do for Yourself," they share something that really stuck with me, and I try to emulate it:

> Do NOT let people invalidate or minimize how you feel. If you feel something, you feel it and it's real to you. Nothing anyone says has the power to invalidate that, ever. No one else occupies your body, or sees life through your eyes. No one else has lived through your exact experiences. And so, no one else has the right to dictate or judge how you feel. Your feelings are important. Never let anyone or any circumstance lead you to believe otherwise.

PERSPECTIVE 6

> Remind yourself that there is a great freedom in leaving others to their opinions, and there is a huge weight lifted when you take nothing personally.[3]

Obviously, easier said than done to ignore the opinions of others, but I always try my best to take a step back and assume that when a response from someone else is harsher than expected, they may be going through something I don't understand.

In my first years of teaching, I struggled tremendously, and I didn't think I would make it past year three. We then had a speaker on opening day who said something that stuck with me: "Never let an eight-year-old ruin your day."

That was me. I was letting eight-year-olds ruin my day, because they were calling me things like "poo-poo head" and everything felt personal.

In that moment, I realized that often those words said to me weren't directed my way. Something else was going on, and I was just the closest person in the way. But I will add something to that gentleman's statement: Never let an eight-year-old, an eighty-year-old, or anyone else in between ruin your day.

We can easily get caught up in the negative thoughts of others when often any change we make in the view of those same people will bring criticism. Some people are critics because of their insecurities or different belief systems. Sometimes they just might not like you and never will. That is a reality.

I struggle with my own (many) insecurities, and when I get caught up in them, I do my best to lift others, not bring them down. It's easy to get caught up in the hamster wheel of negativity, but I know that criticizing others for the sake of doing it empties my self-esteem in the process. I have focused on this belief system: If I had to choose one, I

---

3 Angel Chernoff, "10 Hard Things You Shouldn't Be Afraid to Do for Yourself," Marc & Angel Hack Life, March 16, 2023, accessed November 10, 2025, https://www.marcandangel.com/2023/03/16/dont-be-afraid-to-do-these-10-hard-things-for-yourself/.

would rather be a creator that a critic. Anyone can tear something (or someone) down, but building is the work that I am most interested in doing.

When you need to center your work, consider the following questions:

- What is my purpose?
- How can I serve others?
- How can I build on my strengths?
- How do I learn and identify my shortcomings and mistakes and grow from the process?

The harshest judgment many deal with is self-judgment. Holding ourselves to a high standard is not the same as holding ourselves to an impossible standard. We all falter, and not one person I have ever met is infallible, but it's essential to distinguish between high standards and impossible standards.

Embrace your imperfections, learn from them, and learn from those you care about and who care about you. It will only help you grow.

And don't stop clapping for yourself.

QUESTIONS FOR DISCUSSION

1. Why is it often harder to be kind to ourselves than it is to be kind to others?
2. How can we balance learning from criticism without letting it define our self-worth?
3. What are small ways you can clap for yourself when others don't recognize your efforts?

MOVING FORWARD

EVERY SCHOOL IS A COMMUNITY SCHOOL

"Have you ever worked in a community school?"

This was a question I was asked by a teacher in a workshop only a few weeks before I started writing this book. To be completely transparent, I knew there was more to this question than my initial interpretation, so I requested additional clarification.

"What do you mean by a 'community school'? I am not sure I understand the question."

She clarified by saying, "You just seem to have the philosophy of someone who has worked in a community school, which I currently do, and I was wondering if what you are sharing has been shaped by that experience?"

Now I had a better understanding of what she meant. A "community school" was a distinct entity in education, but I had never formally worked in one.

I asked her to tell me a little bit more about the experience of working in a community school and what that entailed. She shared that a community school (I'm paraphrasing here) does not work in isolation from the community but instead coordinates with them to identify and remove barriers to learning and promote well-being for every child they serve.

As I listened to her, I responded, "While I have never worked for a specific 'community school,' what you just shared should be the norm of what every school is, no matter where they are or their goals."

In the introduction of this book, I shared that most schools aren't about serving the community, but, in reality, many schools *are* the community. I have experienced this as a child going through schools and as an adult working with them.

Growing up in a small town in Canada, as the child of immigrants, I was a member of the only Greek family in the entire town. I remember my sheer embarrassment of my parents speaking in Greek to me in front of my friends and being upset with how they made me feel different from the other kids in the school community.

But then I remember how our school had a cultural heritage night and invited families to share their backgrounds with one another. People were blown away by my parents' story, and what was once embarrassment turned to pride as I realized that people loved the perspectives that my family (and the other families in the community) shared with the school.

My parents would often send food from their Greek restaurant to the school, and the cheers my classmates and teachers shared each time they did made me puff up my chest with the pride I now had in my Greek heritage. To this day I remember at the end of my fourth-grade year, my teacher, Miss Butler, wrote a personalized card to every child, sharing a message of something that stuck out to them. The thing that resonated with me most was she shared how much the room would light up when my parents would send meals for the class, and that it was the first time she had ever had authentic Greek food.

I started to feel like the experience of my family's past was not only something I shouldn't be embarrassed by but something I could embrace in the present to make me better in the future.

In my adulthood, my parents would cook a gigantic meal for every school I ever worked at. Whether or not you liked me before, after eating my mom's baklava, you would love me. My school community didn't push me or anyone to be like everyone else, but it encouraged everyone to bring their gifts and experiences to make the community better.

That was my hope in writing this book. That schools won't be the center of their communities but will become the communities we all hope to have. We often talk about living in a global community, and although that carries some truth, what you do locally can inspire people both locally and globally. This book is a testament to that inspiration.

WE NEED YOUR HELP

It's a Saturday morning, and I'm on a leg machine at the gym. In between sets, I do something that, honestly, I avoid doing while working out. I grab my phone and open up X (Twitter). For the last several years, I try do this as little as possible while at the gym, but for whatever reason, nearing the end of my workout on this day, I open the app and notice this random Tweet (is that what it's called anymore?) from Jesse Fawess:

Jesse Fawess
@fawess211

This is fantastic! Bravo! @gcouros

7:39 AM · 2025-06-28 · **68 Views**

Huh? What did I do that was fantastic? Well, actually nothing. I follow the thread and then see the original post from West Islip Superintendent Dr. Paul Romanelli.

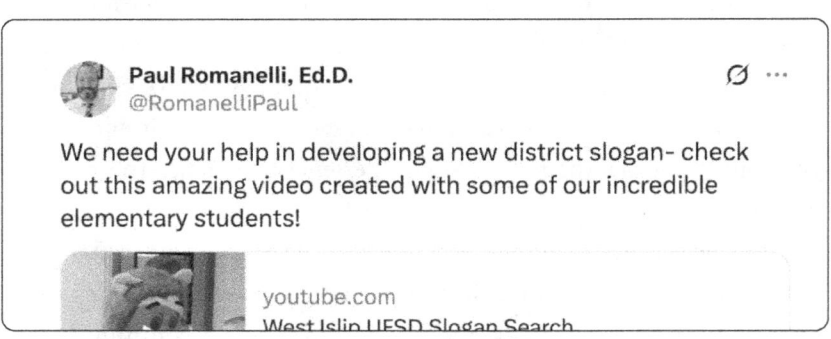

Sparked by curiosity about why Jesse tagged me in the post, I watched the video, and my thirty-second rest between sets turned into three minutes as I viewed the entire thing.

As it begins, you see a group of young children gathered around a table at their last student government meeting of the 2024–2025 school year. The kids are beyond adorable in the video, and they have an increased excitement as they realize Superintendent Romanelli is about to join the meeting.

As he enters the room, the students enthusiastically greet him. Dr. Romanelli says, "We need your help, and quick! We're launching our brand-new website, but we're missing one really big thing: a new slogan."

The kids learn what a slogan is and why it's essential, and similar to the Flight of the Conchords video I discussed earlier in the book, they share some hilarious and cute ideas about what the new slogan should be.

As they put up their own suggestions, the community's lion mascot enters the scene and provides the students some sagely advice: "These are all delectable ideas, but coming up with a slogan is far too tough for only one of seven West Islip schools. Afterall, we're lions. We work together, and we are all about our pride."

The students enthusiastically agree, and then they make an appeal to the greater West Islip community to share their ideas for slogans. To end the video, one of the students shares the following: "Your words could be the first thing everyone sees on our new website. Let's roar together, West Islip!"[4]

After seeing the kids reach out to the adults to build something meaningful, to move forward together, my sweat puddle on the calf machine is now accompanied by tears.

In my emotions, I think, *More of this! We need this more in our schools!*

And then I think, *This is already happening, and there are great schools that are bringing their communities together to build the schools we believe our communities not only need but deserve.*

Inspired by this video, I cancel my afternoon plans, head to Starbucks, and write the first chapter of this book. Instead of complaining about a problem we see in society, I am going to help find a solution and shine light on the solutions already being created, like in the West Islip school community in New York.

I texted and called Dr. Romanelli that Saturday evening and let him know how a random post from a teacher in his community inspired me to write a book. If Jesse had never tagged me in that post, I doubt this book would have ever come to fruition.

A few lessons from this experience: Regardless of your role in the community, you can inspire others to do something great. I didn't hear from the superintendent, Dr. Romanelli, about this initiative, but I heard from a teacher who was inspired by the work in his own district. No matter your role in the community, your actions can inspire others outside your community, but Jesse was also encouraged by his own district. Too often, we see great things from our own people and community and assume they already know they are doing a great job

---

4   "West Islip UFSD Slogan Search," YouTube video, 2:16, posted by West Islip UFSD, March 15, 2025, https://www.youtube.com/watch?v=qfwsCKWCYp0.

and say nothing. If everyone acted that way, though, we would never receive accolades. I have felt that, and it sucks.

That is why, in the very first pages of this book, I shared why it is so essential to tell and create your story together as a community. When Jesse shared the story of his district, I saw the impact of celebrating the success the community had. One story compelled action in me and likely many others. Your stories will have the same effect on others.

Years ago, I committed to telling someone if I see something great or think something extraordinary about them, regardless of how long it's been since we last spoke or the state of our relationship. If you dislike not hearing about the great things you're doing from others, then be the opposite. Be what you want to see in the world. I have never regretted acknowledging the good I have seen in others, but I have regretted *not* saying something.

Secondly, numerous issues exist in education, but many school districts, similar to West Islip, are building the schools they want *with* their communities. We need to spend more time highlighting those examples and how we arrived at that point.

Commack Schools Superintendent Jordan Cox shared the following with me regarding how essential it is to build trust with your entire community, and how that will lead them to go above and beyond, no matter the obstacle:

> The only way to inspire people to go above and beyond, especially during contentious times or when introducing bold, new ideas, is to lead with genuine leadership. That means treating people with dignity and respect.
>
> When you do that, the staff won't just comply, they'll innovate. They'll take risks, step out of their comfort zones, and pour their energy into what's best for children. This only happens when leadership is rooted in trust, respect, and a relentless focus on what's best for children. Leading through change requires not just making the

right decisions for children, but also being fully present to support the people who serve them every day, alongside our community.

The solution is not in reading this book. I am just providing some ideas and perspectives, but I can't actually *do* anything for you. The solution is ultimately what you do to listen, learn, and collaborate to move forward, together.

Finally, you might have picked up this book, read all the way to this final chapter (thanks!), and thought, *We are nowhere near what West Islip is in our community! We can never get there!*

Many have probably picked up this book because they are facing the issues that I have described in these pages. Personally, I would leverage that. Do you know how challenging it is to go into a school or district where everything is going well? That's a tough act to follow!

However, if there are numerous issues, perhaps the only place you can go is up! The same resiliency we ask of our students, we must display ourselves.

Before I sat down to write this final chapter, I heard NBA Hall of Famer Chris Bosh share, "Legends aren't defined by their successes. They're defined by how they bounce back from their failures."[5]

Your school or district might not be where you hoped it would be today, but when we focus on bringing as many people together as possible to move forward, the big winner will not only be your students but also your community.

That is the kind of (school) community I grew up in, and one in which I had the opportunity to thrive because of leaders' high expectations of me and their shared support.

Forward, together.

---

5 "Chris Bosh, Hall of Fame Enshrinement Speech," YouTube video, 34:12, posted by NBA, September 11, 2021, https://www.youtube.com/watch?v=55rxHkBWY38.

May every child and adult have that same blessing of a community working together to create something amazing.

> **QUESTIONS FOR DISCUSSION**
>
> 1. What is one example from your own experience when your school truly felt like a community school? What made that possible? Do others know about this opportunity, and how would they benefit from your sharing?
> 2. How can we better recognize and celebrate the diverse experiences and contributions of families in our school community?
> 3. What is one step you can take this month to strengthen connections between your school and the broader community?

ACKNOWLEDGMENTS

First and foremost, I would like to thank my wife, Paige, for all that she does, for inspiring me to write this book, and for putting an eye on the areas that I am missing to create the best book possible. This book would not be possible without her.

I would also like to thank my children, Kallea, Georgia, and Marino, for constantly reminding me that kids pay more attention to our actions than our words. I want them and every child to have the best opportunities possible for their future. When we work together, that is more likely to happen.

To my parents, who taught me that change is an opportunity to do something amazing and that schools aren't central to community—they are the community. As immigrants to North America, they knew school held the keys to a better life, and they taught me the respect I have for education and educators.

To Meghan Lawson, who walked me through every chapter as I wrote it and challenged and cheered me on throughout the writing process.

Thank you to Dr. Rachel Edoho-Eket for enthusiastically accepting to write the foreword for this book, and for constantly lifting me and so many others to greater heights. Her energy is contagious, and I want to be a better leader and human because of her example.

Katie Martin has been instrumental in all of my books since I first became an author, and she seems to know my voice and what I am trying to say better than I do.

Finally, I want to thank West Islip Schools in Long Island, New York (go Islanders!), Jesse Fawess, and Superintendent Paul Romanelli. If I hadn't been tagged in a post from that community on social media on a Saturday morning, this book would have never happened. Schools all around the world inspire me not only with what is possible in the future, but also with the work they are doing today. With work like this already happening in schools, it is a reminder that you do not need to dream of what is possible—you just need to find it.

ABOUT GEORGE COUROS

George Couros is a worldwide leader in innovative teaching, learning, and leading, with a focus on innovation as a human endeavor.

Most importantly, he is a proud father and husband. His belief that meaningful change happens when you first connect to people's hearts is modeled in his writing and speaking.

In his twenty-plus years in the field of education, he has worked at all levels of school, from K–12 as a teacher, technology facilitator, and school and district administrator. He is currently an adjunct instructor with the Graduate School of Education at the University of Pennsylvania. George is also the author of the books *The Innovator's Mindset: Empower Learning, Unleash Talent, and Lead a Culture of Creativity*; *Innovate Inside the Box: Empowering Learners Through UDL and the Innovator's Mindset;* the Because of a Teacher series, and *What Makes a Great Principal: The Five Pillars of Effective School Leadership*.

George is also the host of the popular education podcast *The Innovator's Mindset.*

He has keynoted hundreds of conferences, including national conferences on five different continents. His work has been translated into multiple languages due to its worldwide impact.

You can learn more about George at
his website, georgecouros.com.

BRING GEORGE COUROS TO YOUR ORGANIZATION OR EVENT!

That was the best speech on any topic
I have ever seen, anywhere.
—Timothy Lambert

Every educator should hear the message George has in his heart! Absolutely life-changing!
—Heather Pennica

George Couros has keynoted hundreds of conferences, including national conferences on five different continents with every part of school communities, including board trustees, district and school leadership, and families and students. His work has been translated into multiple languages due to its worldwide impact. He would love to work with your group!

He speaks on the topic of "Forward, Together: Moving Schools from Conflict to Community During Contentious Times," and other popular engagements include:

- *Embracing Innovation to Help Every Learner Find Success in Their Own Way*
- *Balancing Innovation and Well-Being in Schools*
- *Empowering Parents in the Process of Learning*
- *10 Timeless Principles for Learning, AI, and Emerging Technologies in Education*

To contact and book George to work with your group, please visit georgecouros.com/contact.

MORE FROM GEORGE COUROS

The Innovator's Mindset: Empower Learning, Unleash Talent, and Lead a Culture of Creativity by George Couros

Innovate inside the Box: Empowering Learners Through UDL and Innovator's Mindset by George Couros and Katie Novak

Because of a Teacher: Stories of the Past to Inspire the Future of Education written and curated by George Couros

Because of a Teacher, Volume 2: Stories from the First Years of Teaching written and curated by George Couros

What Makes a Great Principal by George Couros and Allyson Apsey

www.ingramcontent.com/pod-product-compliance
Lightning Source LLC
Chambersburg PA
CBHW050554160426
43199CB00015B/2651